D1196504

WITHDRAWN

A Guide to Non-sexist Children's Books

Volume II: 1976-1985

A Guide to Non-sexist Children's Books

Volume II: 1976-1985

Denise Wilms and Ilene Cooper, Editors

ACADEMY

CHICAGO

Published in 1987 by
Academy Chicago Publishers
425 North Michigan Avenue
Chicago, Illinois 60611

Copyright © 1987 by
Academy Chicago Publishers

Printed and bound in the USA

Library of Congress Cataloging-in-Publication Data

Wilms, Denise.
    A guide to non-sexist children's books,
volume II, 1976-1985.

        Includes indexes.
        1. Children's literature—Bibliography.
2. Sex role in literature—Bibliography.
I. Cooper, Ilene. II. Title.
Z1037.A1W64 1987 [PN1009.A1] 011'.62 86-32262
ISBN 0-89733-161-3
ISBN 0-89733-162-1 (pbk.)

Jacket illustration by Marcia Sewall from SARAH, PLAIN AND TALL by Patricia
MacLachlan. Jacket art copyright © 1985 by Marcia Sewall. Reprinted by permission of Harper & Row, Publishers, Inc.

Acknowledgements

We would like to thank Peter Wilms for technical assistance in compiling the manuscri

We would like to thank the following publishers for illustration reprint permissions:

ATHENEUM PUBLISHERS, INC.

HARPER & ROW, PUBLISHERS, INC.

HOUGHTON MIFFLIN COMPANY

PANTHEON BOOKS, A DIVISION OF RANDOM HOUSE, INC.

VSE PUBLISHER

CONTENTS

Preface IX

Age-Grade Chart X

Pre-School through Third Grade / Fiction 3

Pre-School through Third Grade / Non-Fiction 43

Third Grade through Sixth Grade / Fiction 51

Third Grade through Sixth Grade / Non-Fiction 95

Seventh Grade through Twelfth Grade / Fiction 113

Seventh Grade through Twelfth Grade / Non-Fiction 173

Afterword 193

Small Press Addresses 195

Author Index 197

Title Index 205

Fiction Subject Index 217

Non-Fiction Subject Index 233

PREFACE

Children's literature, like any other literature, is a mirror of its times. In the decade since the first *Guide to Non-Sexist Children's Books* was published, children's books have come to reflect the total life of the child. The picturebooks, novels and non-fiction collected here offer a rich sampling of the diversity and depth found in contemporary children's literature.

Choosing the books was not an altogether easy task; the subject matter of the last decade has given way to the more complex observations of struggle, growth and change that are the constants of real life. The books included in this *Guide* might be best characterized as role-free; many *are* about strong women and forthright young girls, but others are about thoughtful boys or troubled young people of either sex who, through experience and thoughtful observation, learn how to solve their problems independently. That is, after all, what we hope our children of either sex will do.

There are more than six hundred titles included here. For the sake of easy access they have been divided into three broad age groups. Section One features books for the youngest children, those from preschool ages to grade three. Titles for middle grade children appear in Section Two; junior high and high school age readers will find their selections in Section Three. Please remember that these categories are merely general guides, not iron-clad directives; it is the child's interest and ability that should determine the actual choice.

The Editors

AGE-GRADE CHART

Age	Grade
Up to 4	Pre-School
5	Kindergarten
6	1
7	2
8	3
9	4
10	5
11	6
12	7
13	8
14	9
15	10
16	11
17	12

ABBREVIATIONS

O.P.	Out of Print
Gr.	Grade

Pre-School through Third Grade
FICTION

Illustration from NADIA THE WILLFUL by Sue Alexander, illustrated by Lloyd Bloom. Copyright © 1983 by Lloyd Bloom. Published by Pantheon Books, A Division of Random House, Inc.

FICTION

1. Aardema, Verna
   BIMWILI & THE ZIMWI: Ages 5-8
   A TALE FROM ZANZIBAR

   Dial, 1985. $10.89.

   > Based on an African folktale, this picturebook tells
   > the story of a little girl who is captured by a Zimi, an
   > ogre-like creature, but uses her ingenuity to escape.

2. Adler, David
   YOU THINK IT'S FUN   Ages 3-6
   TO BE A CLOWN

   Doubleday, 1980. O.P.

   > Is it fun to be a clown? Farcical stunts may make
   > you think twice, but in the end the answer is yes—at
   > least according to the girl who is revealed without
   > clown makeup at the finish.

3. Adoff, Arnold
   BIG SISTER TELLS ME   Ages 3-6
   THAT I'M BLACK

   Holt, Rinehart & Winston, 1976. $5.95.

   > These bright poems are all about being black and
   > feeling proud. The easy, rhythmic verses work well
   > read aloud and will appeal to preschoolers.

4. _____

UNDER THE EARLY   Ages 6-9
MORNING TREES

Dutton, 1978. O.P.

> A young girl greets the dawn in this lyrical poem.
> Skillfully illustrated with striking black and white
> drawings.

5. Aitkin, Amy
   RUBY!   Ages 5-7

   Bradbury, 1979. $9.95.

> Ruby's daydreams of what she might become when
> she grows up know no bounds. This light story could
> be the basis for discussions of possible careers.

6. Alexander, Sue
   NADIA THE WILLFUL   Ages 7-9

   Pantheon, 1983. $10.95.

> When Nadia loses her beloved brother, her grief is
> alleviated by her enduring memories of him; she is
> able to help her father learn an important lesson
> about love.

7. Aliki
   THE TWO OF THEM   Ages 4-7

   Greenwillow, 1979. $11.25.

> The powerful link between young and old is sensi-
> tively explored in this story of a young girl's relation-
> ship with her grandfather.

8. Allard, Harry
   MISS NELSON IS MISSING   Ages 5-8
   Houghton Mifflin, 1977. $10.95;
   Scholastic paper $1.95.

   MISS NELSON IS BACK
4 Houghton Mifflin, 1982. $8.95.

MISS NELSON HAS A FIELD DAY
Houghton Mifflin, 1985. $12.70.

> Miss Nelson is no one's fool, and when there's a problem at school—unruly children or a losing football team—she knows how to set things straight, with no one the wiser.

9. Bach, Alice
MILLICENT THE MAGNIFICENT   Ages 6-8

Harpor & Row, 1978. $9.57; Dell paper $1.25.

> The relationship between twin bears Oliver and Ronald undergoes a period of tension when Millicent, Girl Wonder of the Wuffiluff's Family Circus, teaches Oliver some fancy tricks that Ronald can't do.

10. Bang, Molly
THE GREY LADY AND THE   Ages 3-5
STRAWBERRY SNATCHER

Macmillan/Four Winds, 1980. $12.95.

> An elderly woman is walking through the forest with her basket of strawberries when a purple creature—the Strawberry Snatcher—appears. The wily old lady outsmarts him and brings the berries home to her family.

11. _____

TEN, NINE, EIGHT   Ages 3-5

Greenwillow, 1983. $10.00.

> This is a counting book and bedtime story rolled into one: a father and daughter share some quiet time as they count the objects in the daughter's bedroom.

FICTION

12. Banish, Roslyn
    I WANT TO TELL YOU   Ages 3-5
    ABOUT MY BABY

    Wingbow Press, 1982; dist. by Bookpeople. $5.95.

    > This simple photo essay deals with the subject of
    > a new baby in the house. A young boy's first-per-
    > son narrative reflects the curiosity, excitement,
    > jealousy, and fears typical of young children ad-
    > justing to the arrival of a new sibling. Both the boy
    > and his father are shown in nurturing roles.

13. Battles, Edith
    WHAT DOES THE   Ages 5-7
    ROOSTER SAY, YOSHIO?

    Albert Whitman, 1978. O.P.

    > A Japanese-speaking boy and an English-speak-
    > ing girl sit on a park bench in America and explore
    > each other's language in this humorous but sensi-
    > tive beginning-to-read book.

14. Bauer, Carolyn Feller
    MY MOM TRAVELS A LOT   Ages 4-7

    Frederick Warne, 1981. $8.95; Puffin paper $3.95.

    > A little girl describes the good things that result for
    > her from her mother's travels—like going out to
    > eat with her dad and getting to stay up late. But
    > there are bad things too—important ones, like
    > missed good-night kisses.

15. Baylor, Byrd
    GUESS WHO MY   Ages 5-8
    FAVORITE PERSON IS

    Scribner, 1977. $7.95.

    > A little farm girl and a grown-up friend trade ideas
    > about their favorite things.

16. Bemelmans, Ludwig
    MADELINE'S CHRISTMAS   Ages 4-6

    Viking/Kestrel, 1985. $12.95.

    > Madeline, who has been taking care of sick
    > teachers and schoolmates, opens the door on
    > Christmas Eve to a rug merchant who turns out to
    > be a magician. He too is ill and Madeline helps
    > him. As a reward, he provides magic carpets
    > which transport everyone home for Christmas.

17. Blaine, Marge
    THE TERRIBLE THING THAT   Ages 5-8
    HAPPENED AT OUR HOUSE

    Macmillan/Four Winds, 1975. $8.95.

    > Everything is topsy-turvy when Mom goes back to
    > work. Her little daughter, who is very angry about
    > it, comes to learn to adjust to the situation.

18. Blegvad, Lenore
    ANNA BANANA AND ME   Ages 5-8

    Atheneum, 1985. $9.95.

    > A timid little boy learns how to come out of his shell
    > by watching his brave and imaginative friend Anna
    > Banana.

19. Blood, Charles L. and Link, Martin A.
    THE GOAT IN THE RUG   Ages 5-7

    Macmillan/Four Winds, 1976. $8.95.

    > Geraldine the goat explains to the reader how
    > Glenmae, a Navajo weaver, turns the wool from
    > Geraldine's coat into a beautiful rug.

20. Buckley, Helen E.
    SOMEDAY WITH MY FATHER   Ages 5-7

    Harper & Row, 1985. $11.89.

    > A little girl describes all the things she is planning
    > to do with her father when—as we see on the last
    > page—her broken leg heals and the cast comes off.

21. Bulla, Clyde Robert
    THE STUBBORN OLD WOMAN   Ages 7-8

    Harper/Crowell, 1980. $9.89.

    > The concerned citizens of a Dutch village send a
    > young girl to convince a stubborn old woman to
    > leave her crumbling house by the river. The persis-
    > tent child finally succeeds in convincing the old
    > lady that everyone will be better off if she moves in
    > with the girl and her orphaned siblings.

22. Burningham, John
    COME AWAY FROM   Ages 5-7
    THE WATER, SHIRLEY
    Harper/Crowell, 1975. $10.53; $3.80 paper.
    Jonathan Cape (London), £3.50; £1.00 paper.

    TIME TO GET OUT OF
    THE BATH, SHIRLEY
    Harper/Crowell, 1978. $10.53.
    Jonathan Cape (London), £3.50.

When Shirley goes to the beach with her parents, she conjures up a pirate ship and finds buried treasure. In the second book, Shirley imagines exciting adventures while she is in her bath.

23. Caines, Jeannette Franklin
    DADDY   Ages 7-8

    Harper & Row, 1977. $9.84.

    A young black girl's Saturdays with her father are a special time. A warm portrait of a nurturing black father.

24. _____

    JUST US WOMEN   Ages 6-8

    Atheneum, 1984. $8.95.

    A little black girl looks forward to the car trip she is going on with her Aunt Martha. They will really enjoy each other's company.

25. Calhoun, Mary
    EUPHONIA AND THE FLOOD   Ages 4-7

    Parents Magazine Press, 1976. O.P.

    In this rollicking picturebook, a country woman named Euphonia sets out with her pig Fatly in her boat Mary Anne to see where her flooded creek is rushing to. Good for reading aloud to groups.

26. Carlson, Nancy
    LOUANNE PIG IN   Ages 3-6
    MAKING THE TEAM

    LOUANNE PIG IN
    THE MYSTERIOUS VALENTINE

    LOUANNE PIG IN
    THE PERFECT FAMILY

LOUANNE PIG IN
THE TALENT SHOW

Carolrhoda Books, 1985. $8.95 each.

> Louanne Pig is a well-adjusted young pig whose adventures in these four books include making the football team, trying to find out who sent her a mysterious valentine, staying at a friend's crowded house on a visit, and discovering that she makes a fine emcee for the school talent show.

27. Carrick, Carol
    THE ACCIDENT   Ages 5-8
    Houghton Mifflin, 1976. $7.95; $3.45 paper.

    THE FOUNDLING
    Houghton Mifflin, 1977. $7.95.

    > These two books examine a child's grief over the death of a pet. In *The Accident*, Christopher deals with the loss of his beloved dog Bodger by allowing himself a good cry. In *The Foundling*, Christopher further recovers from Bodger's death by developing an affection for a puppy who needs a home.

28. _____

    A RABBIT FOR EASTER   Ages 5-7

    Greenwillow, 1979. $11.88.

    > Paul takes his kindergarten's rabbit home with him over Easter vacation. He loses the rabbit when he is distracted by a friend with a new bicycle.

29. Christelow, Eileen
    JEROME THE BABYSITTER   Ages 4-6

    Clarion, 1985; dist. by Ticknor & Fields, $12.95.

Jerome, a young alligator, gets his first babysitting job with the rambunctious Gatorman clan who deliberately try to test his patience.

30. Clifton, Lucille
    EVERETT ANDERSON'S FRIEND   Ages 5-8

    Holt, Rinehart & Winston, 1976. O.P.

    Everett Anderson's new friend in apartment 13A is Maria, a girl who can best Everett at baseball and in a race. But Maria is kind too; she helps Everett when he loses his key and his mother is not at home.

31. _____

    THREE WISHES   Ages 5-7

    Viking, 1976. O.P.

    Zenobia finds a lucky penny on New Year's Day. Will it make her wishes come true? Developments in Zenobia's relationship with her friend Victor show it just might!

32. Coerr, Eleanor
    THE BIG BALLOON RACE   Ages 4-8

    Harper & Row, 1981. $6.95.

    It is 1882 and Ariel's mother is a famous hot air balloonist. Ariel has her own moment of excitement when she is an accidental stowaway during a big race.

33. Cohen, Caron Lee
    SALLY ANN THUNDER   Ages 7-9
    ANN WHIRLWIND CROCKETT

    Greenwillow, 1985. $10.25.

    Tall tales about Davy Crockett's tough wife Sally Ann, who is made of thunder and wears a beehive as a bonnet and a snake as a belt.

11

34. Cohen, Miriam
    JIM MEETS THE THING   Ages 5-8

    Greenwillow, 1981. $11.25.

    Jim worries about being afraid of things that his classmates, both boys and girls, take in stride. But when a praying mantis lands on a boy's coat and scares everyone, Jim is the one who calmly removes it and lets the insect go; afterwards, he realizes that everyone is afraid of something.

35. Craft, Ruth
    CARRIE HEPPLE'S GARDEN   Ages 5-7

    Atheneum, 1979. $9.95.

    Carrie Hepple's garden is a scary place for three children until this unusual old lady invites them in for a special look at "a curiosity or two."

36. Davis, Diane
    SOMETHING IS WRONG   Ages 4-9
    AT MY HOUSE

    Parenting Press, 1984. $3.00.

    This stapled paperback has a dual text aimed at both pre-schoolers and school-age children, to help them cope with emotions caused by domestic violence and to suggest ways they can seek help.

37. Delton, Judy
    A WALK ON A SNOWY NIGHT   Ages 5-7

    Harper & Row, 1982. $9.13.

    A young girl and her father take a walk on a snowy night. Their relationship is warm and close.

38. Delton, Judy, and Knox-Wagner, Elaine
    THE BEST MOM IN THE WORLD   Ages 6-8

    Albert Whitman, 1979. $9.25.

    Lee Henry is angry when his working mother's schedule causes changes that require him to take on some chores. However, he learns that with his help, she can again become the best mom in the world.

39. de Paola, Tomie
    THE LEGEND OF BLUEBONNET: Ages 6-8
    AN OLD TALE OF TEXAS

    Putnam, 1983. $10.95.

    This beautifully illustrated book retells the Comanche legend of the origin of the flower called the bluebonnet. When a young girl bravely sacrifices her beloved doll to bring rain, the gods are pleased and send not only rain, but flowers to her people.

40. _____

    NOW ONE FOOT,   Ages 5-6
    NOW THE OTHER

    Putnam, 1981. $8.95; $3.95 paper.
    Methuen (London), £3.50.

    Bobbie and his grandfather have a close relationship. When Grandfather has a stroke, Bobbie helps him on his road to recovery.

41. _____

    OLIVER BUTTON   Ages 5-7
    IS A SISSY

    Harcourt Brace Jovanovich, 1979. $9.95; $3.95 paper.
    Methuen (London), £3.50; Magnet paper £1.25.

> Because Oliver likes to walk in the woods, to draw and to play-act, he is called a "sissy". But when a local theatre holds a talent show, Oliver shows star quality, and wins the kids' respect.

42. Dickerson, Louise
    GOOD WIFE, GOOD WIFE   Ages 6-8

    McGraw-Hill, 1977. O.P.

    > The young wife in this folktale uses her wits to put her husband's foolish complaining to rest and shows him how to help her care for their new baby.

43. Douglass, Barbara
    GOOD AS NEW   Ages 3-6

    Lothrop, 1982. $11.25.

    > Grady's teddy bear is badly damaged by his little cousin, but it's Grandfather who washes and re-stuffs it, making it more dear than ever.

44. Edelman, Elaine
    I LOVE MY BABY SISTER   Ages 2-5
    (MOST OF THE TIME)

    Lothrop, 1985. $10.50.

    > One of the few "new baby" books about a little girl. This three-year-old likes her baby sister (most of the time) and looks forward to their playing together when the baby is older.

45. Fanshawe, Elizabeth
    RACHEL   Ages 4-7

    Bradbury, 1977. $3.95.
    Bodley Head (London), £2.25.

Rachel is in a wheelchair, but that does not stop her from being very much a part of her class's activities.

46. Farber, Norma
    ALL THOSE MOTHERS   Ages 3-5
    AT THE MANGER

    Harper & Row, 1985. $11.50.

    A warm Christmas poem that calls attention to other mothers at the Christ Child's manger—"hen and cow and mare and ewe"—who welcome the new baby and say, "No mother is a stranger to another anywhere."

47. Gage, Wilson
    MRS. GADDY AND THE GHOST   Ages 3-6
    Greenwillow, 1979. $8.50.

    MRS. GADDY AND THE
    FAST-GROWING VINE
    Greenwillow, 1985. $10.25.

    These are lively comedies about a clever old woman who solves problems with her wits and good humor. In the first story she evicts a ghost; in the second she outwits a vine that won't stop growing by buying a goat that won't stop eating.

48. Galdone, Paul
    THE MAGIC PORRIDGE POT   Ages 3-6

    Houghton Mifflin, 1976. $7.95.

    When Mother can't remember how to stop their magic pot from producing porridge, her little daughter races home to the rescue.

49. Gilchrist, Theo E.
    HALFWAY UP THE MOUNTAIN   Ages 6-8

    Lippincott, 1978; dist. by
    Harper & Row, $8.89.

    > An elderly handicapped couple manage to scare
    > off a bandit and keep his gold in this clever story
    > set in the old world.

50. Goldman, Susan
    GRANDMA IS SOMEBODY SPECIAL   Ages 3-6

    Albert Whitman, 1976. $8.75.

    > A little girl tells about her visit to her grandmother's
    > house. Grandma works, goes to school and some-
    > times even gets mad at Grandpa.

51. Goodall, John
    NAUGHTY NANCY GOES TO SCHOOL   Ages 5-7

    Atheneum, 1985. $9.95.

    > Nancy, an irrepressible young mouse, is a terror
    > at school. But she's also smart, and her quick
    > thinking during her class's seashore outing saves
    > a swimmer who is in trouble.

52. Gordon, Shirley
    THE BOY WHO WANTED   Ages 7-8
    A FAMILY

    Harper & Row, 1980. $9.89;
    Dell paper $1.95.

    > A boy who has been bounced from one foster fam-
    > ily to another finds a good home with an unmarried
    > woman. The relationship is portrayed realistically.

53. Grant, Anne
    DANBURY'S BURNING!   Ages 5-7
    THE STORY OF SYBIL LUDINGTON'S RIDE

    Walck, 1976. O.P.

    > In April of 1777, a Connecticut girl named Sybil
    > Ludington rode on horseback to warn the coun-
    > tryside that the British had come and were burning
    > Danbury.

54. Greenfield, Eloise
    DARLENE   Ages 5-7

    Methuen, 1980. $8.95.

    > Darlene is a little black girl who is confined to a
    > wheel chair. She visits for a few hours with her
    > uncle and cousins at their house and has a good
    > time, playing Monopoly and catch and joining in
    > the family fun.

55. _____

    GRANDMAMMA'S JOY   Ages 5-8

    Putnam/Philomel, 1980. $8.95.

    > A little girl and her grandmother must leave their
    > house because it is too expensive, but Rhondy
    > cheers the old lady up by reminding her that their
    > happiness comes from being together.

56. Grimm, Jacob and Wilhelm
    THE SEVEN RAVENS   Ages 7-8

    Translated by Elizabeth D. Crawford
    Morrow, 1981. $11.25.

    > The classic tale of a young girl's quest to free her
    > seven brothers from an evil spell.

57. Gross, Ruth
    THE GIRL WHO   Ages 4-6
    WOULDN'T GET MARRIED

    Macmillan/Four Winds, 1983. $9.95.

    > An adaptation of a Norwegian folk tale called "The
    > Squire's Bride", in which an unwilling prospective
    > bride deliberately makes herself undesirable in the
    > eyes of the rich farmer who wants to marry her.

58. Hall, Malcolm
    FORECAST   Ages 5-7

    Putnam/Coward-McCann, 1977. O.P.

    > When Stan Groundhog retires as weather
    > forecaster, Caroline Porcupine must prove that
    > groundhogs aren't the only ones who can predict
    > the weather.

59. Hendrickson, Karen
    BABY AND I CAN PLAY   Ages 3-5

    FUN WITH TODDLERS

    Parenting Press, 1985. $3.95 each.

    > These two slim, stapled books explain, through at-
    > tractive charcoal drawings and a smoothly simple
    > text, that children can have lots of fun playing with
    > the babies and toddlers in their families.

60. Hickman, Martha Whitmore
    MY FRIEND WILLIAM   Ages 5-7
    MOVED AWAY

    Abingdon, 1979. $7.95.

    > Jimmy misses the good times he shared with his
    > friend William. But he discovers that he can have a
    > pleasant friendship with Mary Ellen, who lives
    > down the block.

61. Hoban, Lillian
    ARTHUR'S HONEY BEAR   Ages 7-8

    Harper & Row, 1974. $8.61; $2.84 paper.

    > Arthur decides to sell his old toys, but he discovers that he can't bring himself to part with his beloved Honey Bear.

62. Hoff, Sydney
    LITTLEST LEAGUER   Ages 6-8

    Windmill/Dutton, 1976. $2.50 paper.

    > Small, inept Harold is a failure on the ball field until the day Big Leon injures his leg; with teammates and coach shouting their support, Harold turns his size into an asset and saves the day.

63. Howard, Jane R.
    WHEN I'M SLEEPY   Ages 3-5

    Dutton, 1985. $11.95.

    > Lovely illustrations enhance this bedtime story about a little girl who imagines what it would be like to sleep the way animals do.

64. Hughes, Shirley
    GEORGE THE BABYSITTER   Ages 4-7

    Prentice-Hall, 1978. $3.95 paper.

    > A young man named George finds out that babysitting for three lively children is definitely hard work.

65. _____

    UP AND UP   Ages 4-7

    Prentice-Hall, 1978. $9.95; $3.95 paper.
    Bodley Head (London), £3.95; Armada paper £1.00.

    > In this amusing picturebook fantasy, a little girl's

wish to fly becomes reality. She has a great time showing off her new accomplishment.

66. _____

WHEN WE WENT   Ages 1-4
TO THE PARK

Lothrop, 1985. $4.95.

When a little girl and her grandfather go to the park, the things that she sees there constitute a simple preschool counting lesson.

67. Ichikawa, Satomi
FRIENDS   Ages 3-5

Parents Magazine Press, 1977. O.P.

You can do a lot with good friends. In this book boys and girls share secrets, explore meadows and enjoy pillow fights.

68. Isadora, Rachel
BEN'S TRUMPET   Ages 5-9

Greenwillow, 1979. $11.25.

Ben trades his imaginary trumpet for a real one when he is invited to come inside a jazz club where he has been lingering outside and listening for a long time. A Caldecott honor book.

69. _____

MAX   Ages 3-6

Macmillan, 1978. $10.95.

Max has some spare time before a baseball game, so he tags along to his sister's ballet class. There he discovers that dancing is a great way to limber up for a game.

70. Jacques, Faith
    TILLY'S HOUSE   Ages 5-7

    Atheneum, 1979. O.P.

    > Tilly, a maid in a dollhouse, quits her job because
    > she is overworked and nagged by an unpleasant
    > cook. Tilly sets up her own little house in a box on
    > a greenhouse shelf.

71. Jeffers, Susan
    WILD ROBIN   Ages 4-7

    Dutton, 1976. $9.95.

    > A young farm girl named Janet rescues her
    > brother from the fairies in this picturebook which is
    > loosely based on the Scottish ballad "Tamlane."

72. Jewell, Nancy
    BUS RIDE   Ages 6-10

    Harper & Row, 1978. O.P.

    > While she is on a bus going to her grandfather's
    > house, Janie meets Mrs. Rivers, a special new
    > friend.

73. Jonas, Ann
    THE TREK   Ages 4-6

    Greenwillow, 1985. $11.75.

    > On her walk to school, a little girl imagines that she
    > is moving through a dangerous jungle. The first-
    > class illustrations will fascinate young children.

74. Jukes, Mavis
    LIKE JAKE AND ME   Ages 7-9

    Knopf, 1984. $11.95.

    > Alex's new stepfather, Jake, seems big, brave,

and hard to please when it comes to doing "manly" chores like woodchopping. But when a spider frightens Jake and a calm, unafraid Alex helps him out, they gain a deeper appreciation for each other. A Newbery honor book.

75. Kesselman, Wendy
    EMMA   Ages 5-8

    Doubleday, 1980. $7.95.

    This is the story of seventy-two-year-old Emma Stien, who began painting after becoming entranced by a picture she had been given for her birthday. The book is based on a true story.

76. Klein, Norma
    VISITING PAMELA   Ages 4-7

    Dial, 1979. $6.46.

    Five-year-old Carrie is reluctant to visit Pamela's house after school, but by the time her mother comes to pick her up, Carrie is having a good time and has made a new friend.

77. Knotts, Howard
    GREAT-GRANDFATHER,   Ages 6-8
    THE BABY, AND ME

    Atheneum, 1978. O.P.

    After Great-Grandfather talks about how he went to see a new baby when he was a young man, a lonely little boy begins to look forward to meeting his new baby sister.

78. Kroll, Steven
    MRS. CLAUS'S CRAZY CHRISTMAS   Ages 3-5

    Holiday House, 1985. $12.95.

    > When Santa goes off on Christmas Eve and forgets to take one of his important presents, Mrs. Claus hitches a reindeer to an old sleigh and sets off to deliver the gift herself.

79. Langner, Nola
    DUSTY   Ages 6-8

    Coward-McCann, 1976. O.P.

    > A small girl looks after a wild cat which has won her affection. This story conveys a message about a child's need to nurture and an animal's need for independence.

80. Lasky, Katherine
    MY ISLAND GRANDMA   Ages 7-8

    Frederick Warne, 1979. $7.95.

    > As Abbey recalls the summers her family has spent on Grandmother's island off the Maine coast, it becomes clear that Grandmother is someone special.

81. Levinson, Riki
    WATCH THE STARS COME OUT   Ages 5-8

    Dutton, 1985. $12.95.

    > A vivid recreation of an eight-year-old girl's ocean journey from Europe to America at the turn of the century. She and her ten-year-old brother must fend for themselves after the death, during the voyage, of the old woman who has been looking after them.

FICTION

82. Levitin, Sonia
   A SINGLE SPECKLED EGG   Ages 5-6

   Houghton Mifflin/Parnassus, 1976. $6.95.

> In this entertaining story, narrated like a folk tale,
> three clever wives put the worries of their foolish
> husbands to rest.

83. Levy, Elizabeth
   SOMETHING QUEER IS GOING ON   Ages 7-8

   Delacorte, 1973. O.P.; Dell paper, 1982. $1.95.

> In this first book in a series Gwen and Jill are
> friends who solve a number of puzzling mysteries.
> A good choice for children who have progressed
> beyond picturebooks but cannot yet read novels.
> With black and white drawings.

84. Lindsey, Treska
   WHEN BATISTINE MADE BREAD   Ages 4-7

   Macmillan, 1985. $9.95.

> Resourceful little Batistine makes bread from
> scratch on her country farm by harvesting the
> wheat, taking it to the miller and baking the
> dough—all in a day's work.

85. McClenathan, Louise
   MY MOTHER SENDS   Ages 5-7
   HER WISDOM

   Morrow, 1979. $10.95.

> A clever peasant woman outwits a greedy
> moneylender in this original story which is written
> like a folktale.

86. McCully, Emily Arnold
    FIRST SNOW   Ages 3-5

    Harper & Row, 1985. $11.50.

    > A textless picturebook about a large family of mice
    > who celebrate the season's first snow by going to-
    > bogganing. The littlest mouse is afraid to join the
    > fun at first, but she gets up her courage to try and
    > loves it so much she doesn't want to stop.

87. McGovern, Ann
    FEELING MAD FEELING SAD   Ages 3-5
    FEELING BAD FEELING GLAD

    Walker, 1977. $6.95.

    > Children have all kinds of feelings: here are photos
    > of children in varying moods accompanied by free
    > verse expressions of emotion.

88. McLaughlin, Patricia
    THE SICK DAY   Ages 4-6

    Pantheon, 1979. $6.95.

    > When little Emily is too sick to go to school, her
    > father, a writer who works at home, takes care of
    > her. The next day he gets sick and needs to be
    > nursed and amused.

89. McPhail, David
    EMMA'S PET   Ages 2½-4

    Dutton, 1985. $7.95.

    > Emma, a little bear, wants a pet that is big, soft and
    > cuddly. She considers several possibilities and fi-
    > nally settles on her father—the biggest, cuddliest
    > creature of all—who is delighted to be her pet if
    > she will be his.

90. _____

    FARM MORNING   Ages 3-5

    Harcourt Brace Jovanovich, 1985. $12.95.

> A little girl and her father do early morning chores together in the barnyard.

91. Martin, Bill and Archambault, John
    THE GHOST-EYE TREE   Ages 5-8

    Holt, Rinehart & Winston, 1985. $11.95.

> Sent out on a cloudy, windy night for a pail of milk, a little girl and her younger brother must pass the spooky ghost-eye tree. When her brother loses his cap, the sister bravely runs back to retrieve it.

92. Marzollo, Jean
    AMY GOES FISHING   Ages 6-7

    Dial, 1980. $5.89; $2.25 paper.

> Amy's brother and sister tell her that fishing is boring. But she goes fishing with her father anyway and they have a lot of fun.

93. Mayer, Mercer
    LIZA LOU AND THE   Ages 4-8
    YELLER BELLY SWAMP

    Macmillan/Four Winds, 1976. $8.95.

> Cheeky Liza Lou, in the style of Brer Rabbit, gets the best of a variety of threatening creatures in this brightly illustrated picture book.

94. Merrill, Susan
    WASHDAY   Ages 5-7

    Seabury, 1978. O.P.

> Saturday is washday in this nostalgic story, and

everyone, including Papa, participates in the long process that ends with a week's supply of clean clothes for the entire family.

95. Moore, Sheila
SAMSON SVENSON'S BABY   Ages 6-8

Harper & Row, 1983. $9.57.

Samson Svenson, a homely man with a kind heart, carefully nurtures a baby duckling.

96. Munsch, Robert
THE PAPER BAG PRINCESS   Ages 4-6

Annick Press, 1980; dist. by Firefly Books, $10.95; $4.95 paper.

A young princess successfully rescues her boyfriend from a dragon. But when the ungrateful prince then scolds her for looking messy, she tells him exactly what she thinks of him.

97. Murphy, Joan Brisson
FEELINGS   Ages 4-6

Black Moss Press, 1984; dist. by Firefly Books, $5.95.

A little boy who thinks about his feelings decides that although it is certainly good to be happy, it is all right, too, to cry when one is frustrated or sad.

98. Murphy, Shirley Rousseau
TATTIE'S RIVER JOURNEY   Ages 5-8

Dial, 1983. $11.95; $3.95 paper.

Tattie, a young farm woman, welcomes adventure when her house floats down the river in a flood. Along the way, she finds a baby and the gentle young man who will later become her husband.

99. Ness, Evaline
    AMELIA MIXED THE MUSTARD   Ages 5-8

    Scribner, 1975. $7.95.

        A collection of spirited poems about an eclectic batch of heroines. Good-natured fun.

100. Nichol, bp [sic]
     TO THE END OF THE BLOCK   Ages 5-7

     Black Moss Press, 1984; dist. by Firefly Books, $4.95.

        A little girl and her father walk together to the end of their block. An attractive book for children just learning to read.

101. Nolan, Madeena Spray
     MY DADDY DON'T GO TO WORK   Ages 6-8

     Carolrhoda Books, 1978. $5.95.

        A little black girl tells how her family manages while her father is out of work.

102. Oppenheim, Joanne
     MRS. PELOKI'S SNAKE   Ages 5-8

     Dodd Mead, 1980. $9.95.

        Mrs. Peloki is a teacher who is afraid of snakes. When she bravely goes to see if there really is one in the boys' bathroom, she is helped by a little girl who does not share her phobia.

103. Ormerod, Jan
     DAD'S BACK   Ages 1-2

     MESSY BABY

     READING

     SLEEPING

Lothrop, 1985. $4.95 each.

> Daddy looks after his lively baby in these four amusing picturebooks which show a toddler in action.

104. ──────────

101 THINGS TO DO   Ages 3-5
WITH A BABY

Lothrop, 1984. $10.00.

> Everyone, including Daddy, pitches in to help look after this family's busy baby.

105. Ormondroyd, Edward
     JOHNNY CASTLESEED   Ages 5-7

Houghton Mifflin/Parnassus, 1985. $12.95.

> As they walk along the beach, Evan's father tells him about the elusive Johnny Castleseed who makes sand castles. Evan's father builds a sand castle and soon other people on the beach begin to build their own castles. Evan realizes that he and his father are Johnny Castleseeds themselves.

106. Parry, Marian
     I AM A BIG HELP   Ages 3-6

Greenwillow, 1979. $11.25.

> Two little mice help their mother with a variety of household tasks.

107. Pomerantz, Charlotte
     THE HALF-BIRTHDAY PARTY   Ages 5-8

Clarion, 1984; dist. by Ticknor & Fields, $10.95.

> When six-month-old Katie stands up for the first time, her brother Daniel celebrates by giving a half-birthday for her.

108. Porte, Barbara Ann
     HARRY'S MOM   Ages 6-9

     Greenwillow, 1985. $10.25.

     > Harry can't remember what his dead mother was
     > like. He asks his father about her and learns that
     > she was a writer and a daring woman who tried
     > to do everything she wrote about. Harry wonders
     > if he'll ever be as brave as she was. His grandpar-
     > ents reassure him by telling him that his mother
     > was afraid of some things too—and very much
     > like him when she was his age.

109. Quackenbush, Robert
     EXPRESS TRAIN TO TROUBLE   Ages 7-8
     Prentice-Hall, 1981. $8.95.

     CABLE CAR TO CATASTROPHE
     Prentice-Hall, 1982. $8.95.

     STAIRWAY TO DOOM
     Prentice-Hall, 1983. $9.95.

     RICKSHAW TO HORROR
     Prentice-Hall, 1984. $9.95.

     > Miss Mallard is a duck who, like Agatha Chris-
     > tie's Miss Marple, solves mysteries all over the
     > world.

110. Rabe, Bernice
     THE BALANCING GIRL   Ages 7-8

     Dutton, 1981. $10.25.

     > Margaret, a paraplegic, asserts her indepen-
     > dence by balancing things. A conflict arises be-
     > tween her and a boy who does not want to credit
     > her achievements.

111. Ray, Deborah Kogan
     FOG DRIFT MORNING   Ages 5-7

     Harper & Row, 1983. $10.50.

          A mother and daughter walk happily together by
          the sea shortly before dawn in this lyrical little
          book.

112. Rice, Eve
     BENNY BAKES A CAKE   Ages 3-5

     Greenwillow, 1981. $11.25.

          Benny helps his mother bake a birthday cake.
          The dog eats it, but the family refuses to let this
          ruin their celebration.

113. Rockwell, Harlow
     MY NURSERY SCHOOL   Ages 2-5

     Greenwillow, 1976. $11.25; Penguin paper $3.95.

          A positive description of a typical day in a nursery
          school. Fresh, simple illustrations.

114. Rylant, Cynthia
     MISS MAGGIE   Ages 5-7

     Dutton, 1983. $9.95.

          When he first sees her, Nat Crawford is
          frightened of old Maggie Ziegler, but he gets to
          know her and a warm relationship develops be-
          tween them.

115. _____

     THE RELATIVES CAME   Ages 5-7

     Bradbury, 1985; dist. by Macmillan, $12.95.

          In this marvelously evocative story an unnamed
          narrator describes the fun and excitement of
          having a visit from out-of-town relatives.

116. Schertle, Alice
MY TWO FEET   Ages 4-6

Lothrop, 1985. $11.75.

A little girl's lighthearted monologue about all the fun she can have and the places she can go on her own two feet.

117. Schick, Eleanor
HOME ALONE   Ages 7-8

Dial, 1980. $8.89; $3.50 paper.

A little boy must cope with being home alone after school because his mother is working. This book offers strong support to youngsters in this situation.

118. Sendak, Maurice
MAURICE SENDAK'S REALLY ROSIE: Ages 5-8
STARRING THE NUTSHELL KIDS

Harper & Row, 1975. $5.95 paper.

This was a popular television special about a little girl named Rosie who gathers her friends together to make a movie of her life.

119. Sharmat, Marjorie Weinman
EDGEMONT   Ages 5-7

Coward-McCann, 1977. O.P.

Edgemont the turtle is depressed because of his great age until he meets Blanche, a turtle who is even older than he. Her good spirits cheer not only Edgemont, but a crowd of admirers as well.

120. _____

SAY HELLO, VANESSA   Ages 5-7

Holiday House, 1979. $7.95.

> A shy little mouse gathers the courage to speak up and claim her place in her family and in school.

121. _____

TAKING CARE OF MELVIN   Ages 6-8

Holiday House, 1980. $8.95.

> Melvin Dog is so helpful to others that he has no time for himself. But when he falls ill, his friends realize that taking advantage of others' good nature is not a good thing to do.

122. Shecter, Ben
HESTER THE JESTER   Ages 7-8

Harper & Row, 1977. $7.64.

> Hester, a medieval lass, upsets her parents when she announces that she wants to be a court jester like her father.

123. Silverman, Maida
ANNA AND THE SEVEN SWANS   Ages 5-8

Morrow, 1984. $11.50.

> In this adaptation of a Russian fairy tale, Anna's brothers are carried off by a Baba Yaga, a witch. Anna devises an ingenious rescue of the boys with the help of people whom she has helped on her way to the witch's house. Attractively illustrated.

124. Simon, Norma
    I'M BUSY TOO   Ages 4-6

    Albert Whitman, 1979. $9.25.

    > Everyone has a job to do, even young children, whose work may be to go to their day care center. A warm look at the ways in which various family members spend their days.

125. Skorpen, Liesel Moak
    MANDY'S GRANDMOTHER   Ages 5-7

    Dial, 1975. $4.95.

    > Mandy's and Grandmother's expectations of each other cause conflict—until each learns to accept the other's limitations and respect the differences.

126. Smith, Lucia
    MY MOM GOT A JOB   Ages 6-8

    Holt, Rinehart & Winston, 1979. O.P.

    > A little girl thinks about the pros and cons of her mother's having gone to work and about all the adjustments that will have to be made in the household as a result.

127. Snow, Pegeen
    EAT YOUR PEAS, LOUISE!   Ages 5-7

    Children's Press, 1985. $6.50.

    > A determined little girl won't eat her peas until her father says "Please". This simply written book should appeal to pre-schoolers and to first graders just learning to read.

128. Snyder, Carol
    IKE AND MAMA AND THE   Ages 7-9
    ONCE-A-YEAR SUIT

    Coward-McCann, 1978. O.P.

    > In this nostalgic story, set sixty or seventy years
    > ago, Ike's clever Mama contrives to get the best
    > buys in suits for Ike and thirteen other boys in the
    > neighborhood.

129. Spurr, Elizabeth
    MRS. MINETTA'S CAR POOL   Ages 6-8

    Atheneum, 1985. $10.95.

    > Mrs. Minetta's Friday car pool is different from
    > other car pools because the children end up not
    > at school but wherever Mrs. Minetta flies them in
    > her magical automobile.

130. St. George, Judith
    THE HALLOWEEN PUMPKIN SMASHER   Ages 7-9

    Putnam, 1978. $8.95.

    > Who is smashing the Halloween pumpkins?
    > Mary Grace Potts and her imaginary friend Nellie
    > solve a Halloween mystery.

131. Stanley, Diane
    A COUNTRY TALE   Ages 7-9

    Macmillan/Four Winds, 1985. $12.95.

    > Cleo and Nancy, two Victorian cats, are close
    > friends. But they have a falling-out when a weal-
    > thy new neighbor pretends friendship to Cleo
    > and snubs Lucy. Later, when this snobbish cat
    > snubs Cleo too, Cleo learns about the meaning
    > of true friendship.

132. Stecher, Miriam B.
DADDY AND BEN TOGETHER   Ages 6-8

Lothrop, 1981. $11.25.

> When Ben's mother, who is a photographer, leaves town on an assignment, Ben and his father are uncomfortable with each other at first. But after a while they relax and learn to enjoy each other's company.

133. Steptoe, John
DADDY IS A MONSTER...SOMETIMES   Ages 6-8

Lippincott, 1980; dist. by Harper, $9.57; $4.76 paper.

> Two black children discuss their father who, even though they know he loves them very much, turns into a "crazy monster" when they misbehave.

134. Stevens, Carla
ANNA, GRANDPA AND THE BIG STORM   Ages 7-8

Clarion, 1982; dist. by Ticknor & Fields, $7.95.

> It is 1888 and there is a blizzard in New York, but a little girl is determined to get to school because she is a finalist in a spelling bee.

135. Thomas, Jane Resh
ELIZABETH CATCHES A FISH   Ages 7-8

Houghton Mifflin, 1976. $6.95.

> A sensitive portrayal of a little girl's special fishing trip with her father.

136. Turkle, Brinton
RACHEL AND OBADIAH   Ages 6-8

Dutton, 1978. $8.95.

Obadiah and Rachel are Quaker children who live in colonial Nantucket. When a ship safely reaches harbor, Obadiah is sure he can beat Rachel in a race to give the captain's wife the good news. But Rachel surprises him.

137. Tusa, Tricia
     MIRANDA   Ages 6-8

     Macmillan, 1985. $10.95.

     Miranda plays only classical music on the piano, until one day she hears a street musician playing boogie woogie. Miranda then plays only jazz, much to everyone's distress, until she decides she can compromise. Why not, she decides, play both?

138. Van Woerkom, Dorothy
     ALEXANDRA THE ROCK EATER   Ages 5-8

     Knopf, 1978. $7.99.

     Alexandra uses her considerable wit to fool a dragon and gain a cache of gold that will help to support her family of one hundred brothers and sisters.

139. _____

     BECKY AND THE BEAR   Ages 6-8

     Putnam, 1978. O.P.

     In this tale set in Maine in colonial days, Becky is home alone when a bear breaks into her house. Becky dazes him by feeding him a potion laced with rum. Thus she saves herself, and the bear, killed and skinned, provides her family with food, oil and a thick rug.

140. Vincent, Gabrielle
     ERNEST AND CELESTINE   Ages 3-6
     Greenwillow, 1982. $10.25.

BRAVO ERNEST AND CELESTINE
Greenwillow, 1982. $10.75.

ERNEST AND CELESTINE'S PICNIC
Greenwillow, 1982. $10. 75.

MERRY CHRISTMAS, ERNEST AND CELESTINE
Greenwillow, 1984. $11.50.

BREAKFAST TIME, ERNEST AND CELESTINE
Greenwillow, 1985. $5.25.

> Ernest the bear and Celestine the energetic little mouse solve a number of problems in these charming picturebooks.

141. Viorst, Judith
ROSIE AND MICHAEL   Ages 6-8

Atheneum, 1974. $10.95; $2.95 paper.

> An engaging portrait of a friendship between a little girl and boy.

142. Vogel, Ilse-Margaret
DODO EVERY DAY   Ages 7-9

Harper & Row, 1977. O.P.

> Six brief stories about the special feelings between a little girl and her grandmother.

143. Walter, Mildred Pitts
MY MAMA NEEDS ME   Ages 3-6

Lothrop, 1983. $10.00.

> Jason is afraid his mother no longer needs him, so he wants to stay home, ostensibly to help with the new baby. But when she tells him she does need him—for a big hug—he is happy and reassured.

144. Wells, Rosemary
    HAZEL'S AMAZING MOTHER   Ages 4-6

    Dial, 1985; dist. by Dutton, $10.89.

    > When Hazel, a little badger, is waylaid by some rowdy kids, her mother comes to her rescue and sees to it that the bullies receive the kind of justice they deserve.

145. Williams, Vera B.
    A CHAIR FOR MY MOTHER   Ages 5-7

    Greenwillow, 1982. $11.25; $3.95 paper.

    > The heartwarming story of how a grandmother, mother and little granddaughter save up their money to buy a much-needed easy chair for their house.

146. _____

    THREE DAYS ON A RIVER   Ages 4-8
    IN A RED CANOE

    Greenwillow, 1981. $11.25.

    > Two children, the narrator and her cousin Sam, go on an exciting three-day canoe trip arranged by their mothers to introduce them to the pleasures of the great outdoors.

147. Wolde, Gunilla
    BETSY AND THE CHICKEN POX   Ages 3-5
    Random House, O.P.

    BETSY'S FIRST DAY AT NURSERY SCHOOL
    Random House, 1976. $4.95; $1.75 paper.

    > In the first picturebook little Betsy is jealous of the attention her brother gets because he has chicken pox—until she catches it herself. In the second book Betsy, on her first day in nursery

school, gets over her initial fears and plays with the other children.

148. Yeoman, John
THE WILD WASHERWOMEN: Ages 5-8
A NEW FOLK TALE

Greenwillow, 1979. $12.50.

Seven overworked washerwomen rebel, give their stingy employer his comeuppance and find happiness with seven untidy woodcutters.

Pre-School through
Third Grade
NON-FICTION

Illustration from page 22 in HISTORY OF WOMEN FOR CHILDREN by Vivian Sheldon Epstein. Copyright © 1984 by Vivian Sheldon Epstein. Reprinted by permission of VSE Publisher, 212 S. Dexter Street, #51, Denver, Colorado 80222.

NON-FICTION

149. Ancona, George
    HELPING OUT   Ages 3-6

    Clarion, 1985; dist. by Ticknor & Fields, $12.95.

    > In this photo essay boys and girls are shown helping adults with a variety of real work, from raking leaves, to scraping barnacles off a boat, to assisting a glassblower in his shop.

150. Behrens, June
    I CAN BE A TRUCK DRIVER   Ages 6-8

    Children's Press, 1985. $7.95.

    > Part of a career series. In this book both men and women drive trucks for a living.

151. Cole, Joanna
    THE NEW BABY AT YOUR HOUSE   Ages 3-7

    Morrow, 1985. $10.25.

    > This useful book tells what new babies are like, and gives reactions, both positive and negative, of boys and girls who have had to accept new siblings.

NON-FICTION

152. Epstein, Vivian Sheldon
     HISTORY OF WOMEN FOR CHILDREN   Ages 6-10

     Quality Press, 1984. $4.95.

           This social and cultural history of women from
           the beginnings of civilization emphasizes the dif-
           ficulties encountered by women when men
           began to look upon them as property. This book
           is smoothly written, and it is one of the few on
           the subject for young children. It includes lists of
           women who have become successful in various
           fields.

153. Fairfield, Lesley
     LET'S GO!/ALLONS-Y!   Ages 3-6

     Kids Can Press, 1983. $4.95 paper.

           This Canadian book tells in both French and
           English about things that can be seen in places
           where children often go: the library, the doctor's
           office, etc. There are illustrations of both men
           and women working in these places.

154. Girard, Linda
     MY BODY IS PRIVATE   Ages 4-8

     Albert Whitman, 1984. $9.25.

           This book is designed to help young children
           avoid sexual abuse. It explains, in a way that is
           not threatening, that they do not have to allow
           themselves to be physically touched.

155. _____

     WHO IS A STRANGER AND   Ages 4-8
     WHAT SHOULD I DO?

     Albert Whitman, 1985. $9.25.

Protecting their children against kidnapping and sexual abuse is a vital concern of parents. This book gives children important information in a way that is as comfortable as possible, about what to do and what not to do.

156. Gordon, Sol and Gordon, Ruth
A BETTER SAFE THAN SORRY BOOK   Ages 3-6

Ed-U Press, 1984. $5.95 paper.

An attractive, well-written picturebook explaining sexual abuse and how to avoid it in a way that will not frighten children. Included is a section advising parents about discussion of this problem with children.

157. Homan, Dianne
IN CHRISTINA'S TOOLBOX   Ages 3-5

Lollipop Power, 1981. $2.50.

Young Christina uses all sorts of hand tools to build and repair things around the house.

158. Lasky, Kathryn
A BABY FOR MAX   Ages 3-6

Scribner, 1964. $11.95.

The author and her husband, photographer Christopher Knight, record their son Max's reactions to his mother's pregnancy and to the birth of his sister Meribah.

159. Lee, Susan and Lee, John
ABIGAIL ADAMS   Ages 7-9

Children's Press, 1977. O.P.

An interesting introduction to a lively lady, including excerpts from her letters.

160. _____

    ELIZA PINCKNEY   Ages 7-9

    Children's Press, 1977. O.P.

> This strong-willed young woman lived in South Carolina during the eighteenth century, and took charge of her father's plantation when she was sixteen. She experimented with new crops including indigo, the cultivation of which she helped spread throughout the region.

161. Leiner, Katherine
    ASK ME WHAT MY MOTHER DOES   Ages 6-8

    Franklin Watts, 1978. O.P.

> Some of these mothers are doctors and lawyers; some are white collar workers: there is a copywriter and a bank teller, for instance. Still others do blue collar work, like carpentry or steeplejacking.

162. Long, Earlene
    JOHNNY'S EGG   Ages 3-4

    Addison-Wesley, 1980. O.P.

> Breaking open an egg is a challenge to a preschooler. Here a little boy named Johnny successfully cracks an egg without "smashing and squishing all over."

163. Peterson, Jeanne Whitehouse
    I HAVE A SISTER -   Ages 5-7
    MY SISTER IS DEAF

    Harper & Row, 1977. $10.53.

> A little girl explains how her deaf younger sister manages to lead a nearly normal life.

164. Roberts, Maurice
     BARBARA JORDAN: THE GREAT   Ages 7-9
     LADY FROM TEXAS

     Children's Press, 1984. $6.95.

        A short biography of the former Texas Congress-
        woman, with lots of photographs.

165. Rogers, Fred
     GOING TO DAYCARE   Ages 3-5

     THE NEW BABY

     Putnam, 1985. $12. 95 each; $4.95 paper each.

        Photo essays in which the veteran of children's
        television offers good advice to young children
        who face going to daycare or adapting to a new
        baby.

166. Simon, Norma
     ALL KINDS OF FAMILIES   Ages 5-8

     Albert Whitman, 1976. $9.75.

        This book describes some variations of the tradi-
        tional nuclear family, the point being that "people
        who live together, love together, fight together
        and make up, work and play with each other,
        laugh and cry and live under one roof to-
        gether…They are family."

167. Tinkleman, Murray
     COWGIRL   Ages 6-8

     Greenwillow, 1984. $9.00.

        A brief, simple photographic essay about Tracey
        Pearson, who rides her horse to a second-place
        finish in a rodeo barrel-racing contest.

Third Grade through Sixth Grade
FICTION

Illustration from page 93 in HOME by Betsy Gould Hearne, illustrated by Trina Schart Hyman. Illustration copyright © 1979 by Trina Schart Hyman. (A Margaret K. McElderry Book.) Used with the permission of Atheneum Publishers, Inc.

FICTION

168. Adler, C.S.
THE MAGIC OF THE GLITS   Gr. 4-6

Macmillan, 1979. $9.95.

A self-centered twelve-year-old boy, confined by a broken leg, has to look after a nine-year-old girl who is grieving for her mother. There are some tense moments, but eventually the two become friends.

169. _____

THE ONCE IN A WHILE HERO   Gr. 5-7

Coward-McCann, 1982. $8.95.

A polite, thoughtful little boy, who has been called a wimp by the school bully, asks questions about what is feminine and what is masculine behavior.

170. Adoff, Arnold
I AM THE RUNNING GIRL   Gr. 3-5

Harper & Row, 1976. $9.57.

A celebration in free verse of a little girl's track victory and the growing athletic awareness of women in general.

171. Alcock, Vivian
    TRAVELERS BY NIGHT   Gr. 5-8

    Delacorte, 1985. $14.95.

    > When the circus closes down, Bess, a twelve-year-old acrobat and her cousin Charlie, a fellow performer, steal an old elephant to save her from the slaughterhouse.

172. Alexander, Lloyd
    THE WIZARD IN THE TREE   Gr. 4-6

    Dutton, 1975. $9.95.

    > A wizard whose powers are fading gets aid and comfort from a bright kitchen maid named Mallory; together they outwit the villainous Squire Scrupnor.

173. Alter, Judy
    AFTER PA WAS SHOT   Gr. 5-7

    Morrow, 1978. $10.51.

    > This easy-to-read story, set at the turn of the century, is about a girl who discovers that the man her newly-widowed mother has married is a bank robber.

174. Andersen, Hans Christian
    THE WILD SWANS   Gr. 2-5

    Peter Bedrick Books/Harper, 1984. $11.95.

    > A princess uses her ingenuity to rescue her brothers who have been turned into swans.

175. Anderson, Margaret
    JOURNEY OF THE SHADOW BAIRNS   Gr. 5-7

    Knopf, 1980. $8.99.

    > Fourteen-year-old Elspeth has been charged by

her dying mother to care for her four-year-old brother. She and he leave Scotland for Canada, where they will live with relatives.

176. Andrews, Jan, ed.
THE DANCING SUN   Gr. 4-6

Press Porcépic, 1982. $5.95.

This is a collection of short stories and poems about Canadian children from many ethnic backgrounds. One is about an eighteenth-century slave girl who gains freedom by saving her master's fortune while he is in prison; another is a retelling of an Icelandic fairy tale about a shepherd girl who rescues a prince from two female trolls.

177. Asch, Frank
PEARL'S PROMISE   Gr. 4-5

Delacorte/Doubleday, 1984. $12.95; $2.50 paper.

In this suspenseful fantasy Pearl, a white mouse purchased from a pet store, returns to the store to save her brother from becoming a python's next meal.

178. Babbit, Natalie
TUCK EVERLASTING   Gr. 4-6

Farrar, Straus & Giroux, 1975. $10.95;
Bantam paper $2.25.

An interesting tale about a young girl named Winnie Foster, who discovers a dangerous secret and must make some weighty, life-and-death decisions.

179. Barford, Carol
LET ME HEAR THE MUSIC   Gr. 5-8

Seabury, 1979. O.P.

> It is 1940. Twelve-year-old Kathryn Donovan is leading an uneventful existence in a small Wisconsin town, until she makes friends with an orphan named Bennie, who changes her life.

180. Barrington, Elizabeth T.
PART-TIME BOY   Gr. 4-5

Frederick Warne, 1980. O.P.

> Jamie feels uneasy about himself because he is a loner. But when he spends the summer with warm, accepting Maggie, he learns to feel good about himself.

181. Beatty, Patricia
BILLY BEDAMNED, LONG GONE BY   Gr. 5-7

Morrow, 1977. O.P.

> It's 1929 and Merle Tucker's mother is bold enough to take a cross-country automobile trip without her husband. Along the way Merle meets some relatives she's never met before. One of them tells some tales that resolve an old family feud.

182. _____

BY CRUMBS, IT'S MINE   Gr. 5-7

Morrow, 1976. O.P.

> In this lively story, set in 1882, Demaris and her family must support themselves by running a portable tent hotel while Papa searches for gold in the hills of Arizona.

183. _____

JUST SOME WEEDS IN   Gr. 5-7
THE WILDERNESS

Morrow, 1978. O.P.

It is the nineteenth century and Lucinda's family is in dire financial straits because of actions taken by an unscrupulous business partner. But Aunt Adeline Westlake steps in with a new family enterprise and the future looks quite rosy.

184. _____

SOMETHING TO SHOUT ABOUT   Gr. 5-7

Morrow, 1976. O.P.

When the city fathers of a town in Montana in the nineteenth century decide that they will remodel a chicken coop to serve as a school, the townswomen organize and fight for a decent new school building.

185. Beaudry, Jo and Ketchum, Lynne
     CARLA GOES TO COURT   Gr. 3-5

Human Science Press, 1983. $9.95.

When Carla sees a strange man carrying a TV set out of a neighbor's house, she phones the police and is thus responsible for the burglar's eventual arrest.

186. Bellairs, John
     THE HOUSE WITH A CLOCK   Gr. 3-5
     IN ITS WALLS
     Dial, 1973. $10.95; Dell paper $2.75.

     THE FIGURE IN THE SHADOWS
     Dial, 1975. $9.89; Dell paper $2.50.

THE LETTER, THE WITCH AND THE RING
Dial, 1976. $12.95; Dell paper $2.50.

> The hero of this trio of well-written suspenseful books is Lewis, who is shy and overweight, and who is always getting caught up in mysteries which seem to be beyond his abilities. His spunky friend Rose Rita and two benevolent sorcerers—his uncle Jonathan and Mrs. Zimmerman, a neighbor—help him. Rose Rita and Mrs. Zimmerman are most prominent in *The Letter, the Witch and the Ring*.

187. Boutis, Victoria
     KATY DID IT   Gr. 3-5

Greenwillow, 1982. $11.25.

> Katy, a reluctant camper, must put up with the rigors of backpacking in order to spend a weekend with her father.

188. Brady, Esther Wood
     THE TOAD ON CAPITOL HILL   Gr. 4-6

Crown, 1978. $6.95.

> When Dorsey McCurdy's new family is turned topsy-turvy by the War of 1812, she finds herself alone with an ailing stepbrother.

189. _____

TOLIVER'S SECRET   Gr. 4-6

Crown, 1976. $6.95.

> Ten-year-old Ellen disguises herself as a boy in order to take her injured grandfather's place as a courier for General Washington.

190. Brown, Drollene P.
SYBIL RIDES FOR INDEPENDENCE   Gr. 3-5

Albert Whitman, 1985. $9.25.

This is the fictionalization of a true Revolutionary
War story: sixteen-year-old Sybil Ludington's difficult and dangerous ride to alert the Connecticut
countryside that the British had burned Danbury
and were on the march. The book has a good
deal of interesting atmosphere.

191. Brown, Irene Bennett
SKITTERBRAIN   Gr. 5-7

Thomas Nelson, 1978. O.P.

Larnie Moran is a spunky young frontier girl who
needs all the courage she can muster to get the
family cow back when it wanders into a herd of
cattle being driven through some nearby range
land.

192. Bulla, Clyde Robert
SHOESHINE GIRL   Gr. 3-5

Harper/Crowell, 1975. $11.06.

Rebellious young Sara Ida, sent to live with relatives when her mother becomes ill, gets a job
helping to shine shoes and then manages to
keep her employer's shop open after he has
been injured.

193. Burch, Robert
TWO THAT WERE TOUGH   Gr. 4-6

Viking, 1976. $9.95.

A thoughtful, moving story about an older man
whose failing health necessitates his acceding to
his daughter's wishes by leaving the gristmill he
has been operating and moving to the city.

194. Burnett, Frances Hodgson
    SARA CREWE OR WHAT HAPPENED   Gr. 3-5
    AT MISS MINCHIN'S

    Scholastic Paper, 1986; dist. by NAL, $2.25.

    > Written in 1888, this is the story of a poor orphan who goes from one adventure to another.

195. Burstein, Chaya M.
    RIFKA GROWS UP   Gr. 5-7

    Hebrew Publishing Company, 1976. $6.95.

    > A feisty twelve-year-old Jewish girl, caught up in the political and social changes in Russia at the turn of the century, eventually decides to emigrate to America.

196. Byars, Betsy
    CRACKER JACKSON   Gr. 5-7

    Viking, 1985. $11.95.

    > Eleven-year-old Jackson Hunter tries to save his beloved ex-babysitter from an abusive husband. The issues of wife abuse are explored from a child's perspective in this well-written story.

197. _____

    GOODBYE CHICKEN LITTLE   Gr. 5-7

    Harper & Row, 1979. $10.53; Scholastic paper;
    dist. by NAL $1.95.
    Bodley Head (London), £3.25; Puffin paper £.95.

    > When Jimmie's Uncle Pete is killed trying to perform a foolhardy stunt, Jimmie must struggle with his mixed feelings toward his eccentric family.

198. _____

THE NIGHT SWIMMERS   Gr. 5-7

Delacorte, 1980. $9.89; Dell paper $1.75.
Bodley Head (London), £3.95; Puffin paper £1.00.

> While her father, a singer and songwriter, works
> the clubs, young Retta struggles fiercely to care
> for her younger brothers and sisters.

199. _____

THE PINBALLS   Gr. 5 7

Harper & Row, 1977. $10.53; Scholastic paper;
dist. by NAL, $1.95.
Bodley Head (London), £3.75; Puffin paper £1.00.

> While she is living with the Masons, who care for
> abused children, Carlie reaches out to help one
> of her foster brothers, and comes to realize she
> can make choices and need not always be a
> victim.

200. Callen, Larry
SORROW'S SONG   Gr. 4-7

Atlantic Monthly Press, 1979; dist. by Little, Brown. $10.70.

> The small Southern town of Four Corners is the
> setting for this story of a mute girl named Sorrow
> who finds an injured whooping crane and nurses
> it back to health in secret, because some cruel
> townsfolk want to see it captured or on some-
> one's dinner table.

201. _____

WHO KIDNAPPED THE SHERIFF?   Gr. 4-6
TALES FROM TICKFAW

Atlantic Monthly Press, 1985; dist. by Little, Brown. $13.95.

> Eleven-year-old Deever's father is a con man.
> When he leaves town, she goes to stay with the

O'Leary family and, to the dismay of young Pat O'Leary, quick-witted Deever keeps getting the best of him.

202. Calvert, Patricia
HADDER MAC COLL   Gr. 5-8

Scribner, 1985. $12.95.

Set in the Scottish Highlands in 1745, during Bonnie Prince Charlie's uprising against the British, this is the story of brash fourteen-year-old Hadder MacColl, who joins the rebels disguised as a boy.

203. Campbell, Barbara
A GIRL CALLED BOB AND A HORSE   Gr. 4-6
CALLED YOKI

Dial, 1982. $11.95.

In St. Louis during World War II, a black girl named Bob and her friend Chuckie save a grocery cart horse from the glue factory by stealing him. A neighbor helps by sending the horse to her farm. But Bob, who is approaching the time for her baptism, worries about the morality of her actions.

204. Carris, Joan Davenport
WHEN THE BOYS RAN THE HOUSE   Gr. 4-6

Lippincott, 1982; dist. by Harper, $9.57.

While their mother is recuperating from an illness, and their father is in Europe on business, four brothers, the eldest of whom is fourteen, run the household.

205. Child Study Association of America
     COURAGE TO ADVENTURE: STORIES   Gr. 4-6
     OF BOYS AND GIRLS GROWING UP
     WITH AMERICA

     Harper/Crowell, 1976. $10.53.

     > This anthology of songs and stories highlights the bravery of children at critical moments in U.S. history.

206. Clark, Ann Nolan
     ALL THIS WILD LAND   Gr. 5-7

     Viking, 1976. O.P.

     > About one hundred years ago, Maiju and her family, Finnish immigrants, face many hardships as they struggle to build their homestead in Minnesota.

207. Cleary, Beverly
     RAMONA THE BRAVE   Gr. 3-5
     Morrow, 1975; $10.75; Dell paper $2.50.
     Hamish Hamilton (London), £4.50; Puffin paper £1.10.

     RAMONA AND HER FATHER
     Morrow, 1979. $10.75; Dell paper $2.50.
     Hamish Hamilton (London), £5.50; Puffin paper £1.25.

     RAMONA AND HER MOTHER
     Morrow, 1979. $10.95; Dell paper $2.50.
     Hamish Hamilton (London), £5.50; Puffin paper £1.25.

     RAMONA QUIMBY, AGE 8
     Morrow, 1981. $10.25; Dell paper $2.50.
     Hamish Hamilton (London), £5.50; Puffin paper £1.25.

     RAMONA FOREVER
     Morrow, 1984. $9.95.
     Hamish Hamilton (London), £5.50.

     > Children love Ramona. Although in some of the

earlier books women play traditional roles, the heroine of the later books is a solidly realized, independent young girl who, with the support of her imperfect but loving family, learns to weather life's ups and downs.

208. Clifford, Eth
THE REMEMBERING BOX   Gr. 4-6

Houghton Mifflin, 1985. $11.95.

A moving memoir of a Jewish boy's special relationship with his grandmother. He spends the Sabbath with her and she tells him stories about her life in the old country and as a newcomer to America.

209. Clymer, Eleanor
THE GET-AWAY CAR   Gr. 5-7

Dutton, 1978. O.P.

In this comedy-adventure, Aunt Ruby's meddling sends Maggie and her grandmother on a memorable car trip to upstate New York.

210. _____

MY MOTHER IS THE SMARTEST   Gr. 5-7
WOMAN IN THE WORLD

Atheneum, 1982. $8.95.

After Kathleen Rowen and her friend hear the mayor give a speech, they decide that Kathleen's mother, a community activist, could do a far better job than he. She runs for office—and wins.

211. Cohen, Barbara
BENNY   Gr. 5-7

     Lothrop, 1977. $11.88.

          Although Benny Rifkind sees himself as the dumb
          member of his family, he is the one who finds and
          helps a troubled German Jewish boy who has run
          away from home.

212. _____

     THE SECRET GROVE   Gr. 4-5

     Union of American Hebrew Congregations, 1985. $7.95.

          A Jewish and an Arab boy share a brief, secret
          friendship, despite the strife all around them. They
          meet at the common border of their adjacent
          towns.

213. Conford, Ellen
REVENGE OF THE INCREDIBLE
DR. RANCID AND HIS YOUTHFUL
ASSISTANT, JEFFREY

     Little, Brown, 1980. $6.70.

          Eleven-year-old Jeffrey, who is slightly built, is ter-
          rified of the class bully until the day comes when
          Jeffrey must help a friend.

214. Corbett, Scott
HOCKEY GIRLS   Gr. 5-7

     Dutton, 1976. $8.95.

          The prospect of playing hockey does not appeal to
          Irma and her friends, but under the brisk guidance
          of Miss Tingley they discover a spirit they didn't
          know they had.

FICTION

215. Corcoran, Barbara
    THE FARAWAY ISLAND   Gr. 5-7

    Atheneum, 1977. O.P.

    > Lynn, who is very shy, balks at living abroad with her parents while her father is away on a Fulbright scholarship. She elects to stay with her grandmother on Nantucket; there, as her grandmother's problems reveal themselves, Lynn discovers that she is stronger than she thought.

216. Davis, Andrew
    CONRAD'S WAR   Gr. 5-8

    Crown, 1980. O.P.

    > A boy who believes war is a romantic adventure is thrust back in time to World War II and its horrors.

217. Doty, Jean Slaughter
    THE CRUMB   Gr. 4-6

    Greenwillow, 1976. $11.88.

    > This is a mystery for horse lovers about a girl who uncovers a scheme to kill valuable horses in order to collect insurance money.

218. _____

    YESTERDAY'S HORSES   Gr. 4-7

    Macmillan, 1985. $9.95.

    > On a trail ride, Kelly Caldwell finds an odd-looking pony. When Kelly's own horse, Rusty, is stricken by a mysterious virus that has been attacking horses in the region, Kelly's mother, who is a veterinarian, gambles that the mysterious striped pony, which appears to be the last of an extinct breed, will have antibodies that can save Rusty.

219. Dunlop, Eileen
FOX FARM   Gr. 5-7

Holt, Rinehart & Winston, 1979. O.P.

A Scottish boy, who cannot accept the idea that his
father has deserted him, refuses the friendly over-
tures of his foster family. But he comes to change
his attitude when he finds and cares for an orphaned fox.

220. Elmore, Patricia
SUSANNAH AND THE BLUE HOUSE   Gr. 5-7
MYSTERY

Dutton, 1980. $10.25; Archway paper $1.95.

In this interesting mystery, Susannah unravels
the clues that lead her to an old man who has
been missing.

221. Etherington, Frank
THE GENERAL   Gr. 4-6

Annick Press, 1983; dist. by Firefly Books, $5.95;
$2.95 paper.

This story, based on an actual event, is about a
determined young girl who rallies public support
for an unjustly dismissed crossing guard.

222. Feldman, Alan
LUCY MASTERMIND   Gr. 4-6

Dutton, 1985. $10.95.

Lucy Heller has a mind of her own; sometimes
this gets her into trouble, but it also helps to raise
money for a new school bus by organizing a
large dance.

223. Flory, Jane
     THE GOLDEN VENTURE   Gr. 4-6

     Houghton Mifflin, 1976. O.P.

> Staying with the Stanhope family while her father
> prospects for gold, young Minnie and her friends
> work hard to start up a bakery.

224. _____

     THE LIBERATION OF CLEMENTINE   Gr. 4-5
     TIPTON

     Houghton Mifflin, 1974. O.P.

> A lively story about a young girl who declares her
> own independence just as the Philadelphia Cen-
> tennial Exposition of 1876 gets underway.

225. Garrigue, Sheila
     BETWEEN FRIENDS   Gr. 4-6

     Bradbury, 1978; dist. by Macmillan, $9.95.

> Jill's friendship with Dede, a mildly retarded girl,
> conflicts with other interests in her life, but when
> Dede moves to Arizona, Jill realizes what a good
> friend she has lost.

226. Gates, Doris
     A MORGAN FOR MELINDA   Gr. 5-7

     Viking, 1980. $9.95; $3.95 paper.
     Carousel (London), £.95.

> Melissa struggles to overcome her grief over her
> brother's death from leukemia. She becomes the
> owner of a Morgan horse, conquers her fear of
> him and learns to ride, and meets a wise old
> woman writer who teaches her much about
> horses and about life.

227. Gauch, Patricia Lee
THUNDER AT GETTYSBURG   Gr. 3-5

Coward-McCann, 1975. O.P.

> A young girl is caught up in the Battle of Gettysburg when she is sent to help a neighboring family move to a safer place.

228. Giff, Patricia
THE GIFT OF THE PIRATE QUEEN   Gr. 4-6

Delacorte, 1982. $9.95; Dell paper $1.95.

> When young Grace's mother dies, Cousin Fiona comes from Ireland to care for her, bringing marvelous tales of Grania, an Irish pirate queen.

229. _____

LEFT-HANDED SHORTSTOP   Gr. 4-6

Delacorte, 1980. $9.95; Dell paper $1.95.

> A boy who has neither the talent nor the desire to play baseball works hard to help a better player.

230. Gilham, Bill
HOME BEFORE LONG   Gr. 4-6

Andre Deutsch, 1984, dist. by Dutton, $10.06; $1.95.

> Dorothy and her brother are evacuated from South London to Dorset during the air raids of 1940. But the woman they have been placed with is so unpleasant that Dorothy decides they must return to London, no matter how difficult their journey.

231. Goldberger, Judith
THE LOOKING GLASS FACTOR   Gr. 5-7

Dutton, 1979. O.P.

> In the twenty-fifth century, a young girl and two cat companions carry on the research of a scientist whom they think is dead.

67

232. Greaves, Margaret
     A NET TO CATCH THE WIND   Gr. 3-4

     Harper & Row, 1979. $10.89.

> A king who uses his daughter to capture a magical horse is in danger of losing both of them until he realizes that love and freedom are stronger ties than fear and captivity.

233. Greene, Constance
     A GIRL CALLED AL   Gr. 5-7
     Viking, 1969. $10.95; Dell paper $2.25.

     I KNOW YOU, AL
     Viking, 1975. $9.95; Dell paper $2.25.

     YOUR OLD PAL, AL
     Viking, 1979. $10.95; Dell paper $1.95.

     AL (EXANDRA) THE GREAT
     Viking, 1982. $10.95; Dell paper $2.25.

> Alexandra—Al for short—is a likeable, witty heroine. This series follows her through her pre- and early teens.

234. _____

     BEAT THE TURTLE DRUM   Gr. 5-7

     Viking, 1976. $12.50; Dell paper $2.50.

> Kate is close to her sister Joss; when Joss is killed in a sudden accident, Kate must struggle to adjust to life without her sister.

235. Greenwald, Sheila
     THE MARIAH DELANEY LENDING   Gr. 4-6
     LIBRARY

     Houghton Mifflin, 1977. $8.95.

> Young Mariah Delaney's business goes awry when her attempt to start a lending library results

in the loss of some of the most important books belonging to her parents, who are writers and publishers.

236. Griffin, Judith Berry
PHOEBE AND THE GENERAL   Gr. 3-4

Coward-McCann, 1977. O.P.; Scholastic paper $1.50.

During the War for Independence, Phoebe, a young black girl, uncovers a plot to poison General George Washington.

237. Hamerstrom, Frances
WALK WHEN THE MOON IS FULL   Gr. 4-6

The Crossing Press, 1979. $5.95.

Two children, Elva and Alan, hold their mother to her promise to take them on a nature walk each month when the moon is full. These walks provide brief but memorable encounters with wildlife in their natural environment.

238. Harris, Christie
MOUSE WOMAN AND THE   Gr. 5-7
VANISHED PRINCESS

Atheneum, 1976. O.P.

Mouse Woman, a figure from the folklore of the Northwest coast Indians, has a strong interest in children, and gets them out of the trouble they have usually gotten themselves into.

239. _____

THE TROUBLE WITH PRINCESSES   Gr. 5-7

Atheneum, 1980. $9.95.

These Northeast coast Indian tales have strong heroines.

240. Harris, Robie
ROSIE'S RAZZLE DAZZLE DEAL   Gr. 4-5

Knopf, 1982. $4.99; Knopf paper $1.95.

> People think that because Rosie is so cute and nice she can do no wrong; her older brother is usually presumed guilty when something happens. When Rosie breaks a window, she tries to earn money to replace it, but her schemes backfire, and she finally confesses that all the problems were her fault.

241. Hartling, Peter
OMA   Gr. 4-6

Harper & Row, 1977. O.P.

> Kalle is five when he comes to Munich to live with his sixty-seven-year-old grandmother. Despite the difference in their ages, the two develop a strong bond—Oma proves to be one-of-a-kind.

242. Hearne, Betsy Gould
SOUTH STAR   Gr. 3-5
Atheneum, 1977. $7.95.

HOME
Atheneum, 1979. $8.95.

> These two books tell the story of Megan, a giant child cut off from her parents and pursued by a malevolent screamer, a disembodied voice. In *Home*, Megan searches for Brendan, the king of the giants, who has been missing at sea for a long time.

243. Hooks, William
DOUG MEETS THE NUTCRACKER   Gr. 4-6

Frederick Warne, 1977. O.P.

> Doug goes to see his sister dance in *The Nutcracker*, and is carried away with the desire to

become a ballet dancer himself. But he must decide whether he can withstand the inevitable ridicule of his schoolmates when they learn he is taking ballet lessons.

244. Hurwitz, Johanna
BUSYBODY NORA   Gr. 2-4
Morrow, 1976. $8.88; Dell paper $1.50.

NORA AND MRS. MIND-YOUR-OWN-BUSINESS
Morrow, 1977. $8.25; Dell paper $1.25.

NEW NEIGHBORS FOR NORA
Morrow, 1979. $9.50; Dell paper $1.75.

Nora, the likeable little heroine, is full of energy and ideas. In *Busybody Nora*, she is five years old and decides to meet all two hundred of the neighbors who live in her apartment building; in *Mrs. Mind-Your-Own-Business* she copes with a woman who finds her overly friendly and inquisitive; in *New Neighbors* Nora is seven and makes friends with a new boy, although she would much rather have a girl friend.

245. _____

THE LAW OF GRAVITY   Gr. 4-5

Morrow, 1978. $10.51.

A strong mother-daughter relationship is at the core of this sensitive story about a little girl trying to cope with her mother's agoraphobia.

246. _____

MUCH ADO ABOUT ALDO   Gr. 3-4

Morrow, 1978. $10.95.

Eight-year-old Aldo Sossi, an earnest, sensitive boy, loves animals so much that he decides to become a vegetarian.

247. Hutchins, H.J.
      ANASTASIA MORNINGSTAR AND   Gr. 4-6
      CRYSTAL BUTTERFLY

      Annick Press, 1984; dist. by Firefly Books,
      $5.95; paper $2.95.

              A warm friendship grows between a woman with
              extrasensory powers and a strong-willed little
              girl.

248. _____

      THE THREE AND MANY WISHES   Gr. 4-6
      OF JASON REID

      Annick Press, 1983; dist. by Firefly Books,
      $5.95; $2.95 paper.

              Jason is granted three wishes by a gnome
              named Quicksilver. For his first wish, Jason
              chooses a baseball mitt that will improve his
              game. But then he, with the advice of his team-
              mate Penny, uses his remaining wishes in a way
              that will help the whole community.

249. Innocenti, Roberto and Gallaz, Christophe
      ROSE BLANCHE   Gr. 5-7

      Creative Education, 1985. $14.95.

              Sombre in tone, but with stunning illustrations,
              this picturebook for older readers tells the story
              of young Rose Blanche, a German girl who, in
              the midst of the second World War, discovers a
              concentration camp outside her town and risks
              her life by smuggling food to its inmates.

250. Irwin, Hadley
      THE LILITH SUMMER   Gr. 5-7

      Feminist Press, 1979. $8.95.

              Twelve-year-old Ellen and seventy-seven-year-old Lilith are thrown together during a summer holiday and, as a result, a close friendship develops between them.

251. _____

WE ARE MESQUAKIE,   Gr. 5-7
WE ARE ONE

Feminist Press, 1980. $7.95.

While the heroine, a Mesquakie Indian girl, is growing up, her people lose their land in Iowa and must resettle in Kansas.

252. Jacobs, William Jay
MOTHER, AUNT SUSAN, AND ME: Gr. 4-5
THE FIRST FIGHT FOR WOMEN'S RIGHTS

Coward-McCann, 1979. O.P.

A fictional recreation of life in the household of Elizabeth Cady Stanton, the women's rights advocate, told from the point of view of Stanton's daughter Harriot.

253. Karl, Jean
BELOVED BENJAMIN IS WAITING   Gr. 4-6

Dutton, 1978. $10.75.

When her parents desert her, Lucinda Gratz moves into an abandoned house near a cemetery, where she is contacted by intelligent visitors from outer space. This is a basically serious novel with science fictional elements.

254. Kay, Mara
IN THE FACE OF DANGER   Gr. 5-9

Crown, 1977. O.P.

While visiting in Nazi Germany, Ann, an English

girl, comes across two Jewish girls who are hid-
ing in her hosts' attic. Ann befriends the girls and
helps their family to escape from the country.

255. Kaye, Geraldine
COMFORT HERSELF   Gr. 5-7

Andre Deutsch, 1981; dist. by Dutton, $10.95.

When her mother dies, eleven-year-old Comfort
must decide whether to stay on in Ghana with
her father or return to England to live with her
grandparents. The description of cultural differ-
ences in the two countries gives a real substance
to this novel.

256. King-Smith, Dick
THE QUEEN'S NOSE   Gr. 4-6

Harper & Row, 1985. $10.95.

Everyone in Harmony Parker's family hates animals, except Harmony. But when Uncle Ginger
comes visiting from India he gives Harmony a
magic coin that will grant seven wishes for her.
Some of those wishes have to do with her getting
the pet she has always wanted.

257. Klein, Norma
TOMBOY   Gr. 4-6

Macmillan/Four Winds, 1978. $6.95; Archway paper $1.95.

Antonia, a likeable ten-year-old, talks about
everyday incidents that are influencing her de-
velopment into an adult. Among other things she
discusses the effects of sex roles on girls.

258. Kleitsch, Christel and Stephens, Paul
DANCING FEATHERS   Gr. 4-6

Annick Press, 1985; dist. by Firefly Books, $5.95; paper $2.95.

The older women in the Ojibway Indian tribe teach Tafia about her heritage.

259. _____

A TIME TO BE BRAVE   Gr. 4-6

Annick Press, 1985; dist. by Firefly Books, $5.95; paper $2.95.

This story, based on a Canadian film, is told in the first person by a young Ojibway Indian girl whose family spends each winter at their trapping cabin in the Canadian wilderness. When her father is injured, she must screw up her courage and set out for help.

260. Krumens, Anita
WHO'S GOING TO CLEAN UP   Gr. 3-5
THE MESS?

Three Trees Press, 1985. $11.95; $4.95 paper.

The Gunger Family thinks cleaning up is boring, and everyone, including Mother, is too busy to bother. When Mother, an electronics expert, brings home a robot, it too is overwhelmed by the mess. Finally the desperate family comes to realize that if the house is to run smoothly, everyone has to cooperate.

261. Kurelek, William
A NORTHERN NATIVITY: CHRISTMAS   Gr. 5-9
DREAMS OF A PRAIRIE BOY

Tundra Books, 1976. $14.95; $7.95 paper.

In this beautifully illustrated story, a young Canadian boy's dreams of the Holy Family deliver a Christmas message of love and human benevolence.

FICTION

262. Lampman, Evelyn Sibly
      BARGAIN BRIDE   Gr. 5-9

      Atheneum, 1977. $6.95.

           In this story, set in the nineteenth century, fif-
           teen-year-old Ginny is married to a prosperous
           older farmer, through the machinations of her
           greedy relatives. When her husband dies sud-
           denly, Ginny must cope with frontier farming
           and, now that she is a landowner, with un-
           scrupulous suitors.

263. Lane, Carolyn
      GHOST ISLAND   Gr. 4-6

      Houghton Mifflin, 1985. $11.95.

           Four girl campers decide to take a canoe out at
           night and find themselves marooned in the fog
           on nearby Ghost Island, which legend says is
           haunted.

264. Langton, Jane
      THE FRAGILE FLAG   Gr. 5-7

      Harper & Row, 1984. $11.49.

           Georgie, a nine-year-old girl, leads a flag-carry-
           ing, rag-tag procession of kids on a walk from
           Massachusetts to Washington, D.C., where they
           see the President and ask him to stop deploy-
           ment of a nuclear warhead satellite.

265. Lasky, Kathryn
      THE NIGHT JOURNEY   Gr. 5-8

      Frederick Warne, 1981. $8.95.

           Rachel listens, fascinated, as her great-grand-
           mother tells how, as a nine-year-old girl, she
           helped her family escape from Czarist Russia.

266. Layman, Constance
THE GREAT PISTACHIO CASE   Gr. 5-6

Wanderer, 1980. O.P.

> A feisty detective is helped by her granddaughter to find crusty Ophelia Phinney's prize-winning pistachios.

267. Levy, Elizabeth
THE TRYOUTS   Gr. 4-6

Scholastic/Four Winds, 1979. $7.95.

> When girls are allowed to try out for the eighth grade basketball team, two girls make it, causing one player to lose his place. So a confrontation inevitably arises between the kids and the school administration.

268. Lindgren, Astrid
RONIA, THE ROBBER'S DAUGHTER   Gr. 5-6

Viking, 1983. $12.50.
Methuen (London), £5.95.

> This engaging fantasy tells about Ronia, a robber chieftain's independent daughter, whose affection for the son of a rival chieftain brings drastic changes in both their lives.

269. Love, Sandra
BUT WHAT ABOUT ME?   Gr. 4-6

Harcourt Brace Jovanovich, 1976. $8.95.

> Lucy, who is upset when her mother takes a full-time job, begins to develop a sense of independence and responsibility as the family adjusts to the new situation.

270. Lowry, Lois
ANASTASIA KRUPNICK   Gr. 4-6
Houghton Mifflin, 1979. $9.95; Dell paper $2.25.

ANASTASIA AGAIN!
Houghton Mifflin, 1981. $9.95; Dell paper $2.50.

ANASTASIA AT YOUR SERVICE
Houghton Mifflin, 1982. $9.95; Dell paper $2.25.

ANASTASIA, ASK YOUR ANALYST
Houghton Mifflin, 1984. $9.95.

> In this popular series, the inimitable Anastasia
> Krupnick goes from age ten to early adoles-
> cence, coping with a variety of problems, includ-
> ing adjustment to a new sibling and a move from
> an apartment to a house in the suburbs.

271. _____

AUTUMN STREET   Gr. 5-7

Houghton Mifflin, 1980. $8.95.

> When her father is sent to the Pacific during the
> second World War, Elizabeth's family moves in
> with her grandmother, whose house is a fas-
> cinating place.

272. Lurie, Alison
CLEVER GRETCHEN, AND OTHER   Gr. 4-6
FORGOTTEN FOLK TALES

Harper & Row, 1980. $10.89.

> A lively collection of folktales with clever, down-
> to-earth heroines.

273. MacGregor, Ellen and Pantell, Dora F.
MISS PICKERELL TAKES THE   Gr. 3-5
BULL BY THE HORNS

McGraw-Hill, 1976. O.P.

> Miss Pickerell, a determined elderly lady, is angry about a proposed law forbidding ownership of non-cloned animals. She writes to a newspaper about it, and inspires a citizen's campaign against the measure which the governor is about to sign into law.

274. MacLachlan, Patricia
SARAH, PLAIN AND TALL   Gr. 4-6

Harper & Row, 1985. $8.89.

> Anna's prairie home has been lonely for years, ever since her mother died giving birth to Anna's brother Caleb. But when Papa places an ad in the paper for a new wife, Sarah comes to stay and brings a new spirit of love to the family, while retaining her own strong identity. This charming story is set in the nineteenth century. A Newbery Award Winner.

275. _____

THROUGH GRANDPA'S EYES   Gr. 3-4

Harper & Row, 1980. $10.89; $4.09 paper.

> John describes a quiet day at Grandfather's house. Even though Grandpa is blind, he has a special, valuable way of seeing.

276. Mathis, Sharon Bell
THE HUNDRED PENNY BOX

Viking, 1975. $10.95.

> A little black boy's aunt, who is one hundred

years old, uses a box of one hundred pennies to tell him about her life. The illustrations are warm and pleasant.

277. Mauser, Pat Rhoads
A BUNDLE OF STICKS   Gr. 5-7

Atheneum, 1982. $10.95.

Ben sets out to learn an Oriental martial art in order to defend himself against a bully. In the course of his lessons, he also learns about an Eastern philosophy, which tempers somewhat his interest in purely physical dexterity.

278. Mazer, Norma Fox
MRS. FISH, APE, AND ME, THE   Gr. 5-7
DUMP QUEEN

Dutton, 1980. $10.95; Avon paper $2.50.

A trio of town eccentrics, one of them a young girl, band together to help one another in the face of social rejection.

279. Meyers, Bernice
SIDNEY RELLA AND THE GLASS SNEAKER   Gr. 3-5

Macmillan, 1985. $12.95.

A revised version of "Cinderella", in which poor Sidney stays home and cleans while his brothers play football. Sydney's fairy godfather helps him make the team, but he loses his sneaker and must wait for the coach to put it back on.

280. Meyers, Susan
P.J. CLOVER, PRIVATE EYE: THE CASE   Gr. 4-6
OF THE MISSING MOUSE

Dutton/Lodestar, 1985. $11.95.

> In this entertaining mystery, P.J. and her partner, Stacy, get to the bottom of the disappearance of Butch Bigelow's rare Mickey Mouse bank.

281. Miles, Betty
ALL IT TAKES IS PRACTICE   Gr. 5-6

Knopf, 1976. $6.99.

> Stuart Wilson, worried about making new friends, finds he has a lot in common with his basketball-playing neighbor, a girl named Alison.

282. _____

MAUDIE AND ME AND THE   Gr. 5-7
DIRTY BOOK

Knopf, 1980. $7.99; Avon paper $2.25.

> Kate, a schoolteacher, becomes involved in a controversy over an allegedly "dirty" book she has read with her first grade pupils.

283. Minard, Rosemary
LONG MEG   Gr. 3-6

Pantheon, 1983. $8.95.

> Tall and adventurous, Long Meg likes duelling better than working at her father's inn. So she dons male clothing and joins Henry VIII's army in France. This story is based on sixteenth century legends which many scholars believe are about a real woman.

FICTION

284. Moskin, Marietta
    DAY OF THE BLIZZARD   Gr. 3-4

    Coward-McCann, 1978. O.P.

    > Katie sets out to retrieve her mother's brooch
    > from the pawnbroker, but her journey turns out
    > to be more than she bargained for when New
    > York City is hit by the great blizzard of 1888.
    > Katie must depend upon her own resources and
    > some help from strangers in order to get where
    > she is going.

285. Murphy, Shirley Rousseau
    SOONIE AND THE DRAGON   Gr. 3-5

    Atheneum, 1979. O.P.

    > Soonie is a spirited, clever girl who, though left
    > with little but a horse and cart and dog, manages
    > to rescue three princesses, avoid false suitors,
    > and find true love.

286. Naylor, Phyllis Reynolds
    NIGHT CRY   Gr. 4-6

    Atheneum, 1984. $10.95.

    > In the backwoods hill country of Mississippi, thir-
    > teen-year-old Ellen Stump overcomes her great-
    > est fears and saves a life at the same time.

287. Newman, Robert
    THE CASE OF THE BAKER STREET   Gr. 5-7
    IRREGULARS

    Atheneum, 1978. $8.95; $3.95 paper.
    Carousel Books (London), £.85; publ. as *A Puzzle for Sherlock
    Holmes*

    > Andrew arrives in London from his home in
    > Cornwall to find himself in the middle of a mys-

tery. He gets help from Screamer, a plucky little girl, who knows how to get hold of Sherlock Holmes.

288. Nixon, Joan Lowery
CASEY AND THE GREAT IDEA   Gr. 5-7

Dutton, 1980. O.P.; Scholastic paper $1.95.

Casey is twelve years old and a strong upholder of equal rights for women. She helps reinstate a sixty-five-year-old woman as a flight attendant.

289. O'Connor, Jane
YOURS TILL NIAGARA FALLS   Gr. 4-6

Hastings, 1979. $9.95; Scholastic paper $1.95.

Abby is supposed to go to summer camp with her best friend, Merle. But when Merle breaks his ankle and Abby is forced to go to camp alone, she discovers that she can be braver than she thought.

290. O'Dell, Scott
ZIA   Gr. 5-8

Houghton Mifflin, 1976. $11.95.
Oxford University Press (London), £2.95.

Zia, an Indian girl, finds inspiration in her Aunt Karana to strengthen her own struggle aginst the harsh life in a nineteenth-century California Spanish mission. This is a sequel to *Island of the Blue Dolphins*, a Newbery Award winner.

291. Okimoto, Jean Davies
MY MOTHER IS NOT MARRIED TO   Gr. 4-6
MY FATHER

Putnam, 1979. O.P.; Archway paper $1.75.

In this warm, realistic story with touches of

humor, eleven-year-old Cynthia Brown and her six-year-old sister come to accept their parents' separation and divorce.

292. Oxenbury, Helen
THE QUEEN AND ROSIE RANDALL   Gr. 3-4

Morrow, 1979. $10.95.

When the Queen calls Rosie Randall for help, Rosie leaps on her bicycle and rides right over to set things right. This spoof with clever illustrations will amuse this age group.

293. Pascal, Francine
THE HAND-ME-DOWN-KID   Gr. 5-7

Viking, 1980. $9.95; Dell paper $2.25.

Poor Ari Jacobs seems to ba a born loser and a constant victim until a new friend helps her learn how to stand up for herself.

294. Paterson, Katherine
BRIDGE TO TERABITHIA   Gr. 5-8

Crowell, 1977. $10.53; Avon paper $2.25.
Gollancz (London), £5.95; Puffin paper £1.25.

Jesse's life is changed forever by his short friendship with a little girl named Leslie, and by his grief for her when she drowns. Winner of the Newbery Award.

295. _____

THE GREAT GILLY HOPKINS   Gr. 5-7

Harper/Crowell, 1978. $10.53; Avon paper $2.25.
Gollancz (London), £5.95; Puffin paper £1.25.

Gilly, who is eleven years old, bright and rebellious, yearns for the mother who abandoned her when she was three. She rejects Mrs. Trotter, the latest in a series of foster mothers, until

Maime Trotter's unconditional love gets through to her.

296. Pierce, Tamora
ALANNA: THE FIRST ADVENTURE   Gr. 5-7
(SONG OF THE LIONESS, BOOK I)

Atheneum, 1983. $13.95.

Alanna, who wants to be a knight, and her twin brother, who wants to be a sorcerer, change places.

297. Pogrebin, Letty Cotten, ed.
STORIES FOR FREE CHILDREN   Gr. 4-6

McGraw-Hill, 1983. $14.95.

These stories and biographies with strong female role models were compiled to celebrate the tenth anniversary of *Ms* Magazine.

298. Rabe, Bernice
THE GIRL WHO HAD NO NAME   Gr. 5-6

Dutton, 1977. O.P.

Twelve-year-old Girlie solves a family mystery about her father's identity.

299. _____

THE ORPHANS   Gr. 5-7

Dutton, 1978. O.P.

Orphaned twins find a real home with the help of two older women, one of whom is the town sheriff.

FICTION

300. Roche, Patricia K.
    GOOD-BYE, ARNOLD!   Gr. 3-5

    Dial, 1979; dist. by Dutton, $8.50; paper $2.75.

    > At first Webster is happy when his big brother Arnold goes to visit Grandma for a week. Before long, however, he discovers that absence does indeed make the heart grow fonder.

301. Ruckman, Ivy
    WHAT'S AN AVERAGE KID LIKE ME   Gr. 5-7
    DOING WAY UP HERE?

    Delacorte, 1983. $11.95; Dell paper $2.25.

    > When Norman, who is in the seventh grade, decides to save his school, which is on the brink of being closed, his home economics teacher joins the crusade.

302. St. George, Judith
    THE GIRL WITH SPUNK   Gr. 5-7

    Putnam, 1975. O.P.

    > It is 1846 and Josie, a hired girl, hears that the first women's rights convention is being held in Seneca Falls, New York. She does not see the need for this convention, until she has some unhappy but enlightening experiences, including being unfairly dismissed from her job.

303. Selfridge, Oliver G.
    TROUBLE WITH DRAGONS   Gr. 4-6

    Addison-Wesley, 1978. O.P.

    > Three princesses in blue jeans and T-shirts set out to slay a dragon in this tale which turns around traditional fairy story roles.

304. Shreve, Susan Richards
THE BAD DREAMS OF A GOOD GIRL   Gr. 3-5

Knopf, 1982. $8.99; Avon paper $2.25.

>Carlotta is in the fourth grade. She is considered a *good* girl, especially compared to her three unruly brothers. But sometimes Lotty wishes she weren't so well thought of; she must come to terms with her feelings and, in the process, draw closer to her father and her brothers.

305. _____

THE FLUNKING OF JOSHUA T. BATES   Gr. 3-5

Knopf, 1984. $10.95; Scholastic paper $2.25.

>Joshua flunks the third grade. But he grows emotionally while he works hard to rejoin his class.

306. Simon, Marcia L.
A SPECIAL GIFT   Gr. 5-7

Harcourt Brace Jovanovich, 1978. $6.95.

>Eleven-year-old Peter succeeds in getting a part in *The Nutcracker* but he is afraid to acknowledge his love of dancing for fear of being ridiculed by his friends.

307. Simon, Norma
WE REMEMBER PHILIP   Gr. 3-4

Albert Whitman, 1979. $9.25.

>When Sam's teacher's son is killed in a mountain climbing accident, Sam and his classmates extend comfort and sympathy.

308. Singer, Marilyn
    IT CAN'T HURT FOREVER   Gr. 4-6

    Harper & Row, 1978. $10.89; $2.84 paper.

    > Ellie Simon faces heart surgery; while in the hospital she encounters a variety of medical personnel in non-sexist roles.

309. Smith, Doris Buchanan
    SALTED LEMONS   Gr. 4-6

    Scholastic/Four Winds, 1980. $9.95.

    > Darby Bannister, the spunky new girl in town, stands up, during World War II, for a Japanese American friend.

310. Stearns, Pamela
    INTO THE PAINTED BEAR LAIR   Gr. 4-6

    Houghton Mifflin, 1976. O.P.

    > In this engaging fantasy, Sir Rosemary, a female knight, rescues a boy named Gregory from a bear.

311. Stewart, A.C.
    SILAS AND CON   Gr. 4-7

    Atheneum, 1977. O.P.

    > Deserted by his parents, ten-year-old Silas is afraid to trust anyone again until, gradually, he comes to realize that love is a necessity of life.

312. Stoutenburg, Adrien
    WHERE TO NOW, BLUE?   Gr. 5-7

    Macmillan/Four Winds, 1978. O.P.

    > Blueberry Lincoln, twelve years old, makes up her mind to move out of her family's home, where she is unhappy. But she learns the hard way that

she must go back to school and wait to leave home when she is older and better prepared to live on her own.

313. Swede, George
DUDLEY AND THE BIRDMAN   Gr. 2-4

Three Trees Press, 1985. $11.95; $4.95 paper.

Dudley is upset when he learns that an elderly neighbor is trying to trap a songbird and keep it for the winter. He shows the old man how he can hear the bird's beautiful song all winter without taking away its freedom.

314. Terris, Susan
TUCKER AND THE HORSE THIEF   Gr. 5-8

Macmillan/Four Winds, 1979. O.P.

Tucker's father goes off gold prospecting and leaves her to cope in a rough new environment, alone except for her friend Solomon Weil who thinks she's a boy because she dresses like one.

315. Thiele, Colin
THE HAMMERHEAD LIGHT   Gr. 5-7

Harper & Row, 1977. $10.53.
Puffin paper (London), £2.95.

Twelve-year-old Tessa and her elderly friend Alex strive to save an abandoned lighthouse in this vivid story set on the Australian coast.

316. Thomas, Marlo
FREE TO BE YOU AND ME   Gr. 5-7

McGraw-Hill, 1974. O.P.

The poems, songs and stories in this collection are intended to challenge stereotypes and encourage children to be themselves.

317. Thompson, Jean
    DON'T FORGET MICHAEL   Gr. 3-4

    Morrow, 1979. $9.95.

    > Four short stories in which Michael, the youngest child in a large, active family, manages to hold his own and even, sometimes, come out on top.

318. Tolle, Jean Bashor
    THE GREAT PETE PENNEY   Gr. 4-6

    Atheneum, 1979. $8.95.

    > A lively baseball fantasy about Priscilla (Pete) Penney, who, with the help of a six inch high leprechaun and a never-fail curve ball, makes it to the majors.

319. Van Woerkom, Dorothy
    PEARL IN THE EGG   Gr. 4-6

    Harper/Crowell, 1980. O.P.

    > In the Middle Ages, eleven-year-old Pearl and her older brother join a group of wandering minstrels and their fame spreads far and wide.

320. Waldron, Ann
    THE FRENCH DETECTION   Gr. 4-6

    Dutton, 1979. O.P.

    > Wealthy young Bessie Hightower goes to live in France for a month to learn the language. She stays with a young couple, makes new friends and finds herself in the middle of a mystery.

321. _____

    THE LUCKIE STAR   Gr. 4-6

    Dutton, 1977. O.P.

    > Quincy has a scientific bent and is therefore the

odd girl out in her artistic family. During a summer in Florida, she asserts her right to be different.

322. Wallace, Barbara Brooks
     PEPPERMINTS IN THE PARLOR   Gr. 5-7

     Atheneum, 1980. $11.95.

> A recently orphaned girl tries to help the residents of an old people's home, where her aunt works as a cook. Full of suspense.

323. Whitmore, Arvella
     YOU'RE A REAL HERO, AMANDA   Gr. 6-8

     Houghton Mifflin, 1985. $12.95.

> It is the Depression, and Amanda is trying to save her pet, a rooster, from being sent to the country because of a new law barring the keeping of fowl in her town.

324. Williams, Jay
     THE PRACTICAL PRINCESS   Gr. 4-5

     Parent's Magazine Press, 1978. O.P.

> Six fairy tales, in which the heroes and heroines do not behave like stereotypes.

325. Winthrop, Elizabeth
     MARATHON MIRANDA   Gr. 4-6

     Holiday House, 1979. O.P.

> Two girls who live in New York City help each other overcome serious difficulties. Miranda, who is almost thirteen and suffers from asthma, hates any kind of exercise. Her friend Phoebe convinces her to try jogging, helping her to realize that she uses her asthma to cover a fear of failure. Later Miranda helps Phoebe through

the emotional crisis that results when Phoebe
discovers that she is adopted.

326. Yolen, Jane
    THE MERMAID'S THREE WISDOMS   Gr. 4-6

    Collins World, 1978. O.P.

    An angry deaf girl learns from a wise mermaid
    how to accept her disability and get on with life.

Third Grade through Sixth Grade
NON-FICTION

Illustration from page 34 in THE REMEMBERING BOX by Eth Clifford, illustrated by Donna Diamond. Copyright © 1985 by Eth Clifford Rosenberg. Reprinted by permission of Houghton Mifflin Company.

NON-FICTION

327. Adler, David
OUR GOLDA: THE STORY OF GOLDA MEIR   Gr. 3-5

Viking, 1984. $10.95.

> A concise, thoughtful biography of the Israeli prime minister.

328. Arnold, Carolyn
MUSIC LESSONS FOR ALEX   Gr. 3-5

Clarion, 1985; dist. by Ticknor & Fields, $12.95.

> A photo essay about a girl named Alex, who begins to learn to play the violin through the Suzuki method.

329. Asch, Frank and Asch, Jan
RUNNING WITH RACHEL   Gr. 3-5

Dial, 1979. O.P.; $3.95 paper.

> A true story about a girl who gets a good pair of running shoes and some sound advice from an experienced jogger, and sets a goal of becoming a long distance runner.

330. Best, Barbara J.
I LOVE SOFTBALL   Gr. 4-7

Lilac Publishing Co., 1985. $4.25.

> An explanation of the basics of girls' softball, with emphasis on positive attitudes and pure enjoyment of the sport.

331. Blair, Gwenda
LAURA INGALLS WILDER   Gr. 2-4

Putnam, 1981. $6.99; $3.95 paper.

> A biography of the celebrated author whose "Little House" books continue to be popular with new generations of readers.

332. Brown, Fern
RACING AGAINST THE ODDS   Gr. 4-7

    Raintree, 1976. $13.31.

    > An introduction to the life of Robyn Smith, the woman jockey.

333. Clapp, Patricia
I'M DEBORAH SAMPSON: A SOLDIER   Gr. 5-7
IN THE WAR OF THE REVOLUTION

    Morrow, 1977. $11.88.

    > This is an absorbing fictionalized biography of a woman who disguised herself as a man to become a soldier in the War for Independence.

334. Coerr, Eleanor
JANE GOODALL   Gr. 2-4

    Putnam, 1976. O.P.

    > Although it has a fictionalized beginning which is questionable, this book is in the main a straightforward account of this pioneering ethnologist's early career.

335. _____

    SADAKO AND THE THOUSAND   Gr. 3-6
    PAPER CRANES

    Putnam, 1977. $8.95; Dell paper $1.95.

    > A powerful account of the last year of a Japanese girl's life; she was stricken with leukemia ten years after the Bomb was dropped on her city.

336. Davidson, Margaret
THE GOLDA MEIR STORY   Gr. 5-7

    Scribner, 1976. $12.95.

    > Although hampered by fictionalization, this book

shows something of Mrs. Meir's early life, when she had to cope with the traditional attitudes of her parents and her husband.

337. Emberlin, Diane
CONTRIBUTIONS OF WOMEN: SCIENCE   Gr. 5-7

Dillon, 1977. $8.95.

> Profiles of six women scientists: Margaret Mead, Rachel Carson, Lillian Molla Gilbreth, Annie Cannon, Ruth Patrick, and Eugenie Clark.

338. English, Betty Lou
WOMEN AT THEIR WORK   Gr. 3-5

Dial, 1977. O.P.

> Photographs and commentary introduce women in a wide range of employment. Among these are a judge, a carpenter and a sculptor.

339. Faulkner, Margaret
I SKATE   Gr. 5-7

Little, Brown, 1979. $8.95.

> A record, with photos, of the arduous training and psychological stresses undergone by an aspiring woman figure skater.

340. Fooner, Michael
WOMEN IN POLICING: FIGHTING CRIME   Gr. 5-7
AROUND THE WORLD

Coward-McCann, 1976. O.P.

> An interesting international survey of women in police work.

341. Fowler, Carol
DAISY HOOEE NAMPEYO   Gr. 4-6

Dillon, 1977. O.P.

> A biography of a famous Hopi Indian potter, including much information about the Pueblo Indians.

342. Fox, Mary Virginia
JANET GUTHRIE: FOOT TO THE FLOOR   Gr. 5-7

Dillon, 1981. $8.95.

> A biography of a racing car driver.

343.   _____

JUSTICE SANDRA DAY O'CONNOR   Gr. 5-7

Enslow, 1983. $10. 95.

> A straightforward biography of the first woman Supreme Court Justice.

344. Freedman, Russell
ANIMAL FATHERS   Gr. 2-4

Holiday House, 1976. O.P.

> An informative and interesting examination of animal species in which males are the major nurturers of the young.

345. Golden, Flora
WOMEN IN SPORTS: HORSEBACK RIDING   Gr. 4-8

Harvey House, 1978. O.P.

> Profiles of five women equestrians who parlayed their early interest in horses into professional careers.

346. Goldreich, Gloria and Goldreich, Esther
WHAT CAN SHE BE? A COMPUTER   Gr. 3-5
SCIENTIST

Lothrop, 1979. O.P.

> Linda Wong helps theater owners put together a
> computer system that will enable them to track
> ticket sales and plan movie runs.

347. _____

WHAT CAN SHE BE? A FARMER   Gr. 3-5

Lothrop, 1976. O.P.

> This book focuses on two sisters who run a dairy
> farm in Maine.

348. _____

WHAT CAN SHE BE? A   Gr. 3-5
FILM PRODUCER

Lothrop, 1977. O.P.

> Through the activities of film producer Fran
> Sears this interesting book shows how a film is
> supervised from idea to finished product.

349. _____

WHAT CAN SHE BE? A GEOLOGIST   Gr. 3-5

Lothrop, 1976. O.P.

> A look at the career of geologist Ina Brown.

350. _____

WHAT CAN SHE BE? A LEGISLATOR   Gr. 3-6

Lothrop, 1978. $11.35.

> New York politician Carol Bellamy is the subject
> for this look at what a legislator does.

351. Greene, Carol
     MOTHER TERESA: FRIEND OF THE   Gr. 3-5
     FRIENDLESS

     Children's Press, 1983. $10.35.

     > This simply written biography concentrates on Mother Teresa's early life and good works.

352. Greenfield, Eloise
     MARY MC LEOD BETHUNE   Gr. 3-4

     Harper/Crowell, 1977. $10.89.

     > An easy-to-read biography of the distinguished black educator.

353. _____

     ROSA PARKS   Gr. 3-4

     Harper/Crowell, 1973. $10.89.

     > The story of the Alabama black woman whose refusal to move to the back of the bus sparked major civil rights reforms.

354. Gutman, Bill
     WOMEN WHO WORK WITH ANIMALS   Gr. 3-6

     Dodd Mead, 1982. $7.95.

     > Six women who work in traditionally male-dominated fields talk about their jobs: a vet, a zoo keeper, and trainers respectively of horses, dogs, dolphins, and sea lions.

355. Haney, Lynn
     PERFECT BALANCE: THE STORY OF   Gr. 4-6
     AN ELITE GYMNAST

     Putnam, 1979. O.P.

     > This illustrated profile of Olympics aspirant Leslie Russo makes the point that no matter how great

the talent and skill of a gymnast, the future in that field is never certain.

356. Hautzig, Esther R.
LIFE WITH WORKING PARENTS   Gr. 4-6

Macmillan, 1976. $10.95.

A sensible, supportive book for the growing number of children both of whose parents work.

357. Herzig, Alison and Mali, Jane
OH BOY! BABIES!   Gr. 5-7

Little, Brown, 1980. $9.95.

A photo essay about the pleasures and disasters at an infant care class for boys only.

358. Hollander, Phyllis
100 GREATEST WOMEN IN SPORTS   Gr. 5-9

Putnam/Grosset, 1976. O.P.

In addition to tennis, gymnastics and other superstar sports, this book discusses women athletes in lesser known areas of competition like bicycling and volleyball.

359. Hyman, Trina Schart
SELF-PORTRAIT: TRINA SCHART HYMAN   Gr. 4-8

Addison-Wesley, 1981. $8.95.

The author, a well known illustrator of children's books, provides drawings of scenes from her own life.

360. Jacobs, William Jay
ELEANOR ROOSEVELT: A LIFE OF   Gr. 5-8
HAPPINESS AND TEARS

Coward-McCann, 1983. $10.95.

> This well-rounded portrait gives equal weight to Mrs. Roosevelt's childhood, her time in the White House and the successes of her later years. Also suitable for high school age readers.

361. Jones, Betty Milsaps
WONDERWOMEN OF SPORTS   Gr. 3-5

Random House, 1981. $4.99; $3.95 paper.

> The "finest hours" of a dozen outstanding women athletes, among them Nadia Comaneci and Billie Jean King, as well as lesser-known figures.

362. Krementz, Jill
A VERY YOUNG RIDER   Gr. 3-6

Knopf, 1977. $12.95.

> Ten-year-old Vivi Malloy talks about her goal, which is to be a serious horsewoman who some day becomes a member of the U.S. Equestrian team.

363. _____

A VERY YOUNG SKATER   Gr. 3-6

Knopf, 1979. $10.95.

> This hardworking young figure skater wants some day to have her own ice show.

364. Leder, Jane Mersky
     MARTINA NAVRATILOVA   Gr. 4-7

     Crestwood House, 1985. $8.95.

          A brief biography of the tennis player.

365. Lundgren, Hal
     MARY LOU RETTON: GOLD MEDAL   Gr. 2-6
     GYMNAST

     Children's Press, 1985. $6.95.

          A simply written description of the regimen of the
          popular Olympic gymnast. With black and white
          photographs.

366. McGovern, Ann
     NIGHT DIVE   Gr. 5-7

     Macmillan, 1984. $12.95.

          A twelve-year-old girl tells about a nighttime
          scuba dive with her mother, a marine biologist
          who is looking for a certain species of fish.

367. _____

     THE SECRET SOLDIER   Gr. 3-6

     Scholastic/Four Winds, 1975. O.P.;
     Scholastic paper $1.75.

          Deborah Sampson was twenty-two years old
          when she disguised herself as a man so that she
          could fight the British in the Revolutionary War.
          As a result she was one of the first American
          women to travel and give public lectures.

368. Meltzer, Milton
     BETTY FRIEDAN: A VOICE FOR   Gr. 4-6
     WOMEN'S RIGHTS

     Viking/Kestrel, 1985. $9.95.

          A succinct, smoothly-written biography of the

writer whose *Feminine Mystique* helped rekindle the feminist movement in the early sixties.

369. ——————

DOROTHEA LANGE: LIFE   Gr. 4-6
THROUGH THE CAMERA

Viking, 1985. $9.95.

An insightful biography of the photographer whose pictures of the poor and homeless are a memorable documentary of the Depression years.

370. Miller, Margaret
HOT OFF THE PRESS! A DAY AT   Gr. 4-6
THE DAILY NEWS

Crown, 1985. $12.95.

Macy's Thanksgiving Day parade is the event covered in this look at how men and women in various jobs put together a daily newspaper.

371. Morrison, Dorothy Nafus
LADIES WERE NOT EXPECTED   Gr. 5-7

Atheneum, 1977. O.P.

A biography of Abigail Scott Duniway, an Oregon writer and editor, who was a vocal crusader for women's rights in the late nineteenth century.

372. O'Connor, Karen
SALLY RIDE AND THE NEW   Gr. 4-6
ASTRONAUTS: SCIENTISTS IN SPACE

Franklin Watts, 1983. $8.90.

An introduction to the women scientists in the space program.

373. Olney, Ross
     JANET GUTHRIE: FIRST WOMAN   Gr. 4-7
     AT INDY

     Harvey House, 1979. O.P.

         Guthrie, a formidable achiever, not only races
         cars, but has a degree in physics and once
         applied to be an astronaut.

374. Patterson, Lillie
     CORETTA SCOTT KING   Gr. 3-6

     Garrard, 1977. O.P.

         An informative introduction to the wife of the slain
         civil rights leader, an activist in her own right.

375. Phillips, Betty Lou
     PICTURE STORY OF NANCY LOPEZ   Gr. 4-7

     Messner, 1980. O.P.

         A somewhat over-enthusiastic profile of the pro-
         fessional golfer.

376. Saunders, Susan
     DOLLY PARTON: COUNTRY GOIN'   Gr. 4-7
     TO TOWN

     Viking/Kestrel, 1985. $9.95.

         The story of the singer-songwriter who overcame
         poverty and hardship to fulfil her childhood
         dream of becoming a star.

377. Smith, Samantha
     JOURNEY TO THE SOVIET UNION   Gr. 3-7

     Little, Brown, 1985. $19.45; $11.45 paper.

         The late Samantha Smith tells her story.

378. Sobol, Rose
    WOMAN CHIEF   Gr. 5-7

    Dell, 1976. O.P.

            A heavily fictionalized biography of a Crow Indian
            woman who became a warrior and a chief.

379. Sullivan, George
    MARY LOU RETTON: A BIOGRAPHY   Gr. 4-8

    Messner, 1985. $9.29; Wanderer paper $2.95.

            The pressures of competition and instant fame
            are dealt with here, as well as the background
            and training of the gymnast.

380. Terkel, Susan N. and Rench, Janice E.
    FEELING SAFE FEELING STRONG: Gr. 4-6
    HOW TO AVOID SEXUAL ABUSE AND
    WHAT TO DO IF IT HAPPENS TO YOU

    Lerner, 1984. $9.95.

            The authors give sound, vital and supportive ad-
            vice; children needing help are told how and
            where to get it. Discussions include obscene
            phone calls, child pornography, homosexuality
            and rape.

381. Thatcher, Alida M.
    RAISING A RACKET: ROSIE CASALS   Gr. 4-8

    Raintree, 1976. O.P.

            This biography of the former tennis pro includes
            information about her work to improve the status
            of women in tennis.

382. Tinkleman, Murray
    LITTLE BRITCHES RODEO   Gr. 4-6

    Greenwillow, 1985. $11.75.

    > Boys and girls compete in children's rodeo contests held by the National Little Britches Rodeo Association.

383. Tudor, Bethany
    DRAWN FROM NEW ENGLAND: TASHA   Gr. 4-8
    TUDOR. A PORTRAIT IN WORDS AND PICTURES

    Collins World, 1979. O.P.

    > The daughter of the famous illustrator describes her mother's artistic development and her unusual, old-fashioned life in the country. Illustrated with the artist's work and with photographs.

384. Wachter, Oralee
    NO MORE SECRETS FOR ME   Gr. 4-6

    Little, Brown, 1984. $12.45.

    > Four short stories about boys and girls in situations involving some form of sexual abuse. Through the positive actions of the children, youngsters will learn how to avoid such situations or get help if they have not been able to avoid them.

385. Walker, Lou Ann
    AMY: THE STORY OF A DEAF CHILD   Gr. 2-4

    Dutton/Lodestar, 1985. $12.95.

    > Amy, eleven years old, is deaf. Here she talks about her daily activities, showing how in many ways she is like other children, and in a few ways she is different.

NON-FICTION

386. Weiner, Sandra
I WANT TO BE A FISHERMAN   Gr. 3-4

Macmillan, 1977. O.P.

> Christine Vorpahl works alongside her father trap
> fishing; this narrative, illustrated with many black
> and white photographs, explains how they do
> their job.

387. Wilson, Dorothy Clark
I WILL BE A DOCTOR: THE STORY OF   Gr. 5-7
AMERICA'S FIRST WOMAN PHYSICIAN

Abingdon, 1983. $6.95.

> A concise, fictionalized biography of Elizabeth
> Blackwell, describing her childhood, her prog-
> ress through medical school and her work as a
> doctor, educator and social worker.

388. Wolf, Bernard
ANNA'S SILENT WORLD   Gr. 3-4

Lippincott, 1977; dist. by Harper, $12.45.

> Anna is deaf, but with special training and strong
> family support, she is able to enjoy a nearly nor-
> mal life. With photographs.

389. _____

CONNIE'S NEW EYES   Gr. 5-7

Lippincott, 1975; dist. by Harper, $12.45.
Archway paper $1.75.

> A photo essay about a young teacher who gets a
> seeing eye dog.

390. Woods, Harold and Geraldine
EQUAL JUSTICE: A BIOGRAPHY OF   Gr. 5-7
SANDRA DAY O'CONNOR

Dillon, 1985. $9.95.

> An introduction to the first woman U.S. Supreme Court Justice, appointed in 1981 by Ronald Reagan. Also suitable for high school age readers.

391. Zeck, Gerry
I LOVE TO DANCE: A TRUE STORY   Gr. 3-5
ABOUT TONY JONES

Carolrhoda Books, 1983. $8.95.

> Ten-year-old Tony Jones is a male student at a dance school in Minneapolis.

392. Zemach, Margo
SELF PORTRAIT: MARGO ZEMACH   Gr. 4-5

Addison-Wesley, 1978. $12.95.

> A well-known children's book illustrator describes in words and pictures how she became an artist.

Seventh Grade through Twelfth Grade
FICTION

Illustration from page 27 in CLEVER GRETCHEN And Other Forgotten Folktales by Alison Lurie, illustrated by Margot Tomes. Illustration copyright © 1980 by Margot Tomes. Reprinted by permission of Harper & Row, Publishers, Inc.

FICTION

393. Aaron, Chester
 DUCHESS   Gr. 7-9

 Lippincott, 1982; dist. by Harper, $10.10.

> The life of a delinquent boy changes when he is sent to his uncle's sheep ranch, where he finds and trains a mongrel dog.

394. Adler, C.S.
 ROADSIDE VALENTINE   Gr. 7-10

 Macmillan, 1983. $9.95.

> A seventeen-year-old boy, torn between his father and his need to be independent, gets emotional support from a girl he wants to win away from her macho boyfriend.

395. Alexander, Lloyd
 WESTMARK   Gr. 7-10
 Dutton, 1981. $11.95; Dell paper $2.50.

 THE KESTREL
 Dutton, 1981. $10.95; Dell paper $2.75.

 THE BEGGAR QUEEN
 Dutton, 1984. $11.95; Dell paper $2.95.

> A compelling, wittily written trilogy that begins with a revolution and ends with the various revolutionary factions at each others' throats. At the center of the storm is Mickle, a resourceful, intelligent young woman who was a beggar but is now a queen.

396. Allan, Mabel Esther
 THE MILLS DOWN BELOW   Gr. 6-9

 Dodd Mead, 1981. $7.95.
 Abelard Schuman (London), £3.95.

> Feminism is at the heart of this story of wealthy,

sheltered Elinor Rillsden, who comes to resent and protest her Victorian father's iron-fisted rule of his family and his weaving mills (which employ primarily women and children).

397. _____

A STRANGE ENCHANTMENT   Gr. 7-10

Dodd Mead, 1982. $8.95.
Abelard Schuman (London), £4.95.

Prim wants to help the British war effort in World War II, but at sixteen she's to young to join the army. So, she signs up for the Women's Land Army and learns farming, an occupation she comes to enjoy.

398. _____

THE VIEW BEYOND MY FATHER   Gr. 7-8

Dodd Mead, 1978. O.P.
Abelard Schuman (London), O.P.

Mary Anne Angus, a blind girl who eventually partially regains her sight, fights for a measure of independence from her protective parents.

399. Anderson, Margaret
LIGHT IN THE MOUNTAIN   Gr. 6-9

Knopf, 1982. $9.99.

A story of the Maris, a Polynesian tribe, seen through the eyes of two strong priestesses.

400. Angell, Judie
SECRET SELVES   Gr. 6-9

Macmillan/Bradbury, 1979. $9.95; Dell paper $1.75.

In this comic light romance, a girl has opinions about women which differ considerably from those of the boy on whom she has a crush.

401. _____

TINA GOGO   Gr. 6-9

Macmillan/Bradbury, 1978. $9.95; Dell paper $2.50.

Foster child Tina Gogo's brassy exterior covers a soft heart. After spending a summer with foster parents in a small resort town, Tina decides to return home to care for her ailing mother.

402. Baehr, Patricia
FAITHFULLY, TRU   Gr. 7-9

Macmillan, 1984. $11.95.

In this absorbing story of family relationships, Tru must try to find her father, whom she thought was dead, and initiate a dialogue with her uncommunicative mother.

403. Barger, Gary
WHAT HAPPENED TO MR. FORSTER   Gr. 5-8

Clarion, 1981; dist. by Ticknor & Fields, $8.95.

Louis Lamb's confidence is bolstered because of the kindly supportiveness of his teacher, Mr. Forster. When Forster is fired for being a homosexual, Louis is naturally upset and must sort through a range of emotions.

404. Barkhouse, Joyce
THE WITCH OF PORT LAJOYE   Gr. 6-8

Ragweed Press, 1983. $8.95 paper.

This story, part of the oral tradition of the Micmac Indians, is about a young Basque woman of Prince Edward Island who, because she had learned the natural medicine practiced by the Micmacs, was burned as a witch by settlers in the early eighteenth century.

405. Beatty, Patricia
THAT'S ONE ORNERY ORPHAN   Gr. 6-8

Morrow, 1980. $10.51.

This is the colorful story, set in nineteenth-century Texas, of recently orphaned Hallie Lee Baker's efforts to find a new home with a suitable family.

406. _____

TURN HOMEWARD HANNALEE   Gr. 6-8

Morrow, 1984. $10.25.

As a punishment for making cloth for the Confederacy, Hannalee and a host of other Georgia textile workers are shipped to Indiana by General Sherman to labor in Northern factories. Hannalee promises her mother that she will return, and despite great hardships, she keeps her word.

407. Beatty, Patricia, and Beatty, John
MASTER ROSALIND   Gr. 7-9

Morrow, 1974. O.P.

This lively mystery-adventure set in Elizabethan times is about a sharp-witted girl named Rosalind who is kidnapped but escapes and joins the company of players at the Globe Theatre.

408. Beckman, Delores
MY OWN PRIVATE SKY   Gr. 6-8

Dutton, 1980. $9.95.

Arthur's new sixty-eight-year-old babysitter turns out to be an inspiring and enthusiastic treasure. Because of her, Arthur learns to feel comfortable with himself and to conquer his fear of the water so that he can learn to swim.

409. Bess, Clayton
BIG MAN AND THE BURNOUT   Gr. 7-9

Houghton Mifflin, 1985. $12.95.

When Jess develops an unexpected friendship with the class tough guy, he discovers they have much in common and learns some important lessons about friendship and caring for others.

410. _____

STORY FOR A BLACK NIGHT   Gr. 6-12

Houghton/Parnassus, 1982. $7.95.

Set in the Liberian bush two generations ago, this is a powerful short novel about a woman who admits two travellers with a sick baby to her hut for shelter. When they abandon the baby, who has smallpox, she makes a painful moral decision to care for the child—at terrible cost to herself and her family.

411. Bethancourt, T. Ernesto
DORIS FEIN: SUPERSPY   Gr. 9-12

Holiday House, 1980. $10.75.

This is the first in a growing series of books about Doris Fein, a feisty young private detective from southern California who roams the world solving mysteries.

412. Bierhorst, John
     THE HUNGRY WOMAN: MYTHS AND   Gr. 7-10
     LEGENDS OF THE AZTECS

     Morrow, 1984. $9.50.

          In this carefully edited collection there are sev-
          eral stories about powerful women.

413. Blos, Joan
     A GATHERING OF DAYS: A NEW ENGLAND   Gr. 6-8
     GIRL'S JOURNAL, 1830-32

     Scribner, 1979. $10.95; $3.50 paper.

          Winner of the Newbery Award, this is an histori-
          cal novel written in the form of entries in a journal
          by a thirteen-year-old New England girl in the
          1830s. Absorbing details provide a sense of what
          life was like for a hardworking, religious family. In
          the course of the story, Catherine Hall aids a
          runaway slave, mourns the death of her best
          friend, and adjusts to her widowed father's re-
          marriage.

414. Bogen, M. Arthur
     BARELY UNDERCOVER   Gr. 9-12

     Avon/Flare, 1983. $2.25.

          Grant and his karate-proficient girlfriend pose as
          thieves to learn who has made a retarded friend
          take a robbery rap.

415. Bond, Nancy
     THE BEST OF ENEMIES   Gr. 6-8

     Atheneum, 1978. $9.95.

          In this contemporary story, set in Concord, Mas-
          sachusetts, twelve-year-old Charlotte becomes
          involved in a plan to save a local Patriot's Day
          celebration from disruption when a group of visit-

ing Englishmen actually want to re-fight the historic battle at Concord Bridge.

416. _____

COUNTRY OF BROKEN STONE   Gr. 6-9

Atheneum, 1980. $12.95.

Fourteen-year-old Penelope must adapt to many changes in family situations, to a new friend whose background is different from her own, and to her own desire for time alone to draw and think. This English story has especially well-drawn characters and a worthwhile message.

417. _____

A PLACE TO COME BACK TO   Gr. 7-9

Atheneum, 1984. $12.95.

Fifteen-year-old Charlotte helps her friend Oliver come to terms with his grandfather's death.

418. _____

A STRING IN THE HARP   Gr. 7-9

Atheneum, 1976. $13.95.

In this fantasy, the Morgans adjust to the death of their mother as they settle into a Welsh community, where twelve-year-old Peter discovers an ancient harp key that draws him into the past and an intriguing mystery.

419. Boyd, Candy Dawson
BREADSTICKS AND BLESSING PLACES   Gr. 6-8

Macmillan, 1985. $11.95.

Toni Douglas, an adolescent black girl from a middle class family, is devastated by the death of her best friend Susan, who was run down by a drunken driver. Her grief seems uncontrollable until her friend Mattie, who had lost her father, gives Toni an idea that helps her come to grips with her feelings.

420. Branfield, John
THE FOX IN WINTER   Gr. 7-12

Atheneum, 1982. $11.95.
Gollancz (London), £5.95; Armada paper £1.25.

A teen-aged girl and her mother, a district nurse, help an ailing old man in the last year of his life. Set in England.

421. Branscum, Robbie
TOBY, GRANNY AND GEORGE   Gr. 6-8
Doubleday, 1977. $7.95.

TOBY ALONE
Doubleday, 1979. $7.95.

TOBY AND JOHNNY JOE
Doubleday, 1979. $7.95.

This trio of slim novels is set in the Arkansas hill country, where Toby and her beloved Granny scratch out a living on their mountain farm. The stories follow Toby from girlhood to womanhood, during which time Granny dies, Toby marries, goes through World War II, and welcomes home a husband who has lost his leg.

422. Brenner, Barbara
THE GORILLA SIGNS LOVE   Gr. 9-12

Lothrop, 1984. $9.50.

Based on the work of primate researchers, this is the appealing story of an eighteen-year-old girl who teaches the American Deaf Sign Language to a gorilla.

423. Bridgers, Sue Ellen
ALL TOGETHER NOW   Gr. 7-9

Knopf, 1979. $7.99.

During the summer, Casey Flanagan's father goes off to fight in the Korean War and her mother takes a job. But she appreciates her ties to a handful of close friends and relatives.

424. Briggs, Katherine Mary
KATE CRACKERNUTS   Gr. 6-8

Morrow/Greenwillow, 1980. $13.75.
Kestrel (London), O.P.

The seventeenth-century English used here demands able readers, but those who try will find a strong story about a quick-thinking young girl who defies a sorcerer mother to protect her stepsister.

425. Brooks, Jerome
THE BIG DIPPER MARATHON   Gr. 7-12

Dutton, 1979. $1.75 paper.

Fifteen-year-old Ace Zweig, crippled by polio, learns to deal with his well-meaning but misguided parents and to establish a new self-image.

426. Brown, Irene Bennett
ANSWER ME, ANSWER ME   Gr. 7-11

Atheneum, 1985. $13.95.

Eighteen-year-old Bryn Kinney, using clues found among her deceased grandmother's possessions, travels to a small town in Kansas, hoping to discover her own hitherto mysterious origins.

427. _____

> BEFORE THE LARK   Gr. 6-8
>
> Atheneum, 1982. $10.95.
>
>> It is 1888, and plucky twelve-year-old Jocey
>> Royal and her ailing grandmother move to Kan-
>> sas where Jocey has the backbreaking task of
>> farming the land while at the same time seeking
>> an operation to repair her harelip.

428. Brown, Marion Marsh
> HOMEWARD THE ARROW'S FLIGHT   Gr. 5-8
>
> Abingdon, 1980. O.P.
>
>> A fictionalized biography of Susan La Flesche,
>> an Omaha Indian who encountered discrimina-
>> tion in her successful undertaking to become the
>> first doctor of her race in the United States. Set in
>> the late nineteenth century.

429. Burchard, Peter
> CHINWE   Gr. 6-9
>
> Putnam, 1979. O.P.
>
>> Chinwe and her younger brother, held aboard a
>> slave ship bound for Cuba, plot a mutiny. But
>> when the ship runs aground near St. Simon's Is-
>> land off the coast of Georgia, they are enslaved
>> once more.

430. Cameron, Eleanor
> A ROOM MADE OF WINDOWS   Gr. 5-7
> Dutton, 1971. $10.95.
>
> JULIA AND THE HAND OF GOD
> Dutton, 1977. $9.95.
>
> THAT JULIA REDFERN
> Dutton, 1982. $9.95.

JULIA'S MAGIC
Dutton, 1984. $10.95.

> Julia Redfern is the earnest, likeable heroine in this quartet of books. She is introduced as an adolescent in *A Room Made of Windows* and then each succeeding volume moves back in time to describe her upbringing and development.

431. Cavanna, Betty
RUNAWAY VOGAGE   Gr. 6-8

Morrow, 1978. O.P.

> Tired of being an indentured servant to an unpleasant Boston family, fifteen-year-old Eliza Foster dares to stowaway aboard a ship taking women to frontier Seattle. Based on an actual 1866 voyage.

432. Cebulash, Mel
RUTH MARINI OF THE DODGERS   Gr. 6-9
Lerner, 1983. $8.95.

RUTH MARINI: DODGER ACE
Lerner, 1983. $8.95.

RUTH MARINI WORLD SERIES
Lerner, 1984. $8.95.

> The heroine of these novels begins to have success in sports in high school and eventually achieves fame as a baseball superstar.

433. Chambers, John
THE COLONEL AND ME   Gr. 7-9

Atheneum, 1985. $11.95.

> Gussie McPherson discovers she has a true talent for horseback riding under the firm and sometimes abrasive tutelage of Colonel Meslenko.

123

434. Childress, Alice
WHEN THE RATTLESNAKE SOUNDS: Gr. 7-12
A PLAY

Coward-McCann, 1975. O.P.

> This smoothly crafted one-act play is about Harriet Tubman's influence on two young girls involved in the Underground Railroad.

435. Cleaver, Vera
SWEETLY SINGS THE DONKEY   Gr. 6-9

Harper & Row, 1985. $12.50.

> Lily has more common sense than her irresponsible parents. When the family moves to Florida to claim inherited land, her father becomes ill and her mother deserts them both. So it is Lily who oversees the building of the house.

436. Cleaver, Vera and Bill
HAZEL RYE   Gr. 6-8

Harper & Row, 1983. $11.06.

> Hazel, a forthright Florida girl, has no goals until the industrious Poole family comes to her orange grove seeking work. They settle into a little house on her property and eventually she comes to appreciate their hard work and ambition.

437. _____

QUEEN OF HEARTS   Gr. 6-8

Lippincott, 1978; dist. by Harper, $10.95.

> Wilma's stay with her ailing grandmother triggers confrontation and then a positive solution to what Wilma recognizes as Granny's fear of losing her independence.

438. _____

TRIAL VALLEY   Gr. 6-9

Lippincott, 1977; dist. by Harper, $10.95.
Oxford University Press (London), £2.95.

> This sequel to *Where the Lilies Bloom (see Guide, Volume I),* takes up Mary Call and her family two years later. Mary Call is weighed down by her responsibilities and is worried about her future as she deals with an abandoned child and two suitors.

439. Clements, Bruce
ANYWHERE ELSE BUT HERE   Gr. 6-8

Farrar, Straus & Giroux, 1980. $9.95; Dell paper $1.95.

> Thirteen-year-old Molly Smelter wants to leave Schenectady where her father's printing business has failed. She persuades her father to move to Connecticut and start another print shop.

440. Clifford, Eth
THE ROCKING CHAIR REBELLION   Gr. 7-8

Houghton Mifflin, 1979. $8.95.

> Fourteen-year-old Opie goes to work at a home for the aged and finds more excitement than she expected. She becomes involved with the fight that several of the residents are waging to live by themselves in a home they have bought; they are opposed by local residents.

441. Cohen, Barbara
BITTER HERBS AND HONEY   Gr. 7-9

Lothrop, 1976. $11.88.

> In 1916 Becky Levitsky must balance the wishes

of her Orthodox Jewish family with her own desire for an education and a better life for herself.

442. Cohen, Barbara and Lovejoy, Bahija
SEVEN DAUGHTERS AND SEVEN SONS   Gr. 7-9

Atheneum, 1982. $10.95.

Buran, the cleverest daughter of a poor Baghdad shopkeeper, leaves home disguised as a young man in order to restore her father's fortune and outwit her scornful uncle, the father of seven sons. She becomes a successful merchant, doing better than her seven cousins, who all fail in business, and she is sought after by a Tyrian prince who has learned that she is a woman.

443. Collier, James Lincoln and Collier Christopher
WAR COMES TO WILLY FREEMAN   Gr. 7-9

Delacorte, 1983. $12.95.

A free young black girl who has lost both parents in the War for Independence must make her own way without being captured and sold back into slavery. A vivid depiction of the situation of both women and blacks in America in the Revolutionary era.

444. _____

WHO IS CARRIE?   Gr. 6-9

Delacorte, 1984. $14.95.

Carrie, an irrepressible eighteenth-century kitchen slave, fights to solve the mystery of her parentage.

445. Collura, Mary Ellen Lang
WINNERS   Gr. 7-9

Western Prairie Books, 1984. $7.95 paper.

> Jordy, a Blackfoot Indian, was orphaned as a child and placed in a string of foster homes. Now in his teens, he is sent to live with his grandfather, who has just been released from prison. Grandfather's cabin on the reservation is the first real home Jordy has had in a long time. Among other things, he helps a determined blind girl learn to ride. Several of the characters here are strongly independent women.

446. Colman, Hila
RACHEL'S LEGACY   Gr. 7-12

Morrow, 1979. $10.95.

> Set in turn-of-the-century New York City, this book traces the life of Rachel Ginsburg, who comes to America at a young age with her mother and two sisters. As a young woman she goes into the tailoring business and makes a success of it.

447. Conford, Ellen
STRICTLY FOR LAUGHS   Gr. 7-10

Putnam/Pacer, 1985. $12.95.

> Joey Merino has two goals—she wants to be a comedienne and she wants Peter Stillman to be her boyfriend. In this amusing story she achieves both goals.

448. ⎯⎯⎯⎯⎯

WHY ME?   Gr. 6-9

Little, Brown, 1985. $12.95.

> G.G. Graffman, a bright, attractive girl who wants to be a marine biologist, has a crush on Hobie

and Hobie knows it. But he's more interested in beautiful, blonde and empty-headed Darlene. Hobie learns the hard way that there is more to love than looks. By the time he's ready for G.G., she may no longer be interested in him.

449. Conrad, Pamela
PRAIRIE SONGS   Gr. 6-10

Harper & Row, 1985. $11.50.

The moving story of beautiful, fragile Emmeline, a doctor's wife who cannot endure life on the Nebraska Plain in the nineteenth century. Young Louisa, the narrator of the story, and Louisa's mother, are contrasted with Emmeline; they are strong, capable women, the kind who helped build the West.

450. Cooney, Caroline B.
I'M NOT YOUR OTHER HALF   Gr. 7-10

Putnam/Pacer, 1984. $10.95.

Can seventeen-year-old Fraser live her life and maintain a relationship with a possessive boy-friend as well?

451. Cooper, Susan
OVER SEA, UNDER STONE   Gr. 6-9
Atheneum, 1965. $10.95; $4.95 paper.
Puffin paper (London), £1.25.

THE DARK IS RISING
Atheneum, 1974. $13.95; $2.95 paper.
Chatto & Windus (London), £4.95; Puffin paper £1.25.

GREENWITCH
Atheneum, 1974. $13.95; $2.95 paper.
Chatto & Windus (London), £4.95; Puffin paper £1.25.

THE GREY KING
Atheneum, 1975. $10.95; $3.50 paper.
Chatto & Windus (London), £4.95; Puffin paper £1.25.

SILVER ON THE TREE
Atheneum, 1977. $11.95; $2.95 paper.
Chatto & Windus (London), £4.95; Puffin paper £1.35.

> This is a quintet of fantasies concerned with the clash between good and evil. The central character for the most part is eleven-year-old Will Stanton, who learns he is one of the Old Ones, and that he must unite the forces of light to do battle against the gathering forces of darkness.

452. Corcoran, Barbara
    "ME AND YOU AND A DOG NAMED BLUE"   Gr. 7-9

    Atheneum, 1979. O.P.

> Athletic fifteen-year-old Maggie Clark isn't sure about anything except baseball—someday she wants to play on a professional women's team. Her dream is sidetracked when she attracts the interest of a socialite dog-breeder who not only wants her to work at her kennels, but tries to run the girl's life, until Maggie puts her foot down.

453. Cresswell, Helen
    ORDINARY JACK   Gr. 6-8
    Macmillan, 1977. $9.95; Avon paper $1.50.
    Puffin paper (London), £1.25.

    ABSOLUTE ZERO
    Macmillan, 1978. $9.95; Avon paper $1.75.
    Faber & Faber (London), £5.95; Puffin paper £1.25.

    BAGTHORPES UNLIMITED
    Avon paper, 1978. $1.75.
    Faber & Faber (London), £5.95; Puffin paper £1.10.

BAGTHORPES VS THE WORLD
Macmillan, 1979. $9.95.
Faber & Faber (London), £5.95; Puffin paper £1.25.

THE BAGTHORPES ABROAD
Macmillan, 1984. $10.95.
Faber & Faber (London), £5.95.

> These are five hilarious books about a distinctly idiosyncratic family whose members—mother, father, three daughters and two sons—are convinced they are brilliant; each tries to outdo the others at everything they undertake.

454. Cross, Gillian
ON THE EDGE   Gr. 6-9

Holiday House, 1985. $10.95.

> A perceptive young girl in rural Derbyshire notices that something is amiss in the cottage that some strangers have rented for a holiday. Realizing that the boy she has seen there is the kidnapped son of a well-known BBC figure, she becomes involved in an intricate plan to trap the terrorists who hold him. Above average suspense.

455. Cunningham, Julia
TUPPENY   Gr. 7-10

Dutton, 1978. O.P.; Avon paper $1.95.

> In this sober, meditative book, the presence of a strange young girl deeply affects three couples who have had unhappy relationships with their daughters.

456. Davis, Gibbs
FISHMAN AND CHARLY   Gr. 6-8

Houghton Mifflin, 1983. $8.95.

> Eleven-year-old Tyler, whose mother has recently died, sets out to swim across the bay to im-

press his father. Tyler runs across manatee poachers and tries to protect a pregnant manatee.

457. Dixon, Paige
WALK MY WAY   Gr. 6-10

Atheneum, 1980. $7.95.

A fourteen-year-old girl goes on a cross-country walk in order to avoid her abusive, alcoholic father and thus takes control of her own life.

458. Dodd, Wayne
A TIME OF HUNTING   Gr. 6-9

Houghton Mifflin, 1975. $6.95.

A young Oklahoma boy comes to realize that he cannot hunt: the emotional price he pays is too high. While the message is implicitly anti-hunting, the book is not strident but quietly powerful.

459. Duncombe, Frances Riker
SUMMER OF THE BURNING   Gr. 6-9

Putnam, 1976. O.P.

Thirteen-year-old Hannah must grow up before her time when the War for Independence claims her father, and her mother dies in childbirth. In taking over family responsibilities, she faces a tough future; how she successfully copes provides an absorbing and convincing tale.

460. Dygard, Thomas
REBOUND CAPER   Gr. 7-10

Morrow, 1983. $9.50.

When a class clown is suspended from his team for showing off on the basketball court, he joins the girls' basketball team as a joke, only to find this is not as funny as he thinks it will be.

461. Eige, Lillian E.
THE KIDNAPPING OF MISTER HUEY   Gr. 6-8

Harper & Row, 1983. $9.57.

A sensitive boy befriends an energetic old man
and helps to keep him out of a nursing home.

462. Ellis, Ella Tharp
HUGO AND THE PRINCESS NENA   Gr. 6-8

Atheneum, 1983. $10.95.

When an eleven-year-old girl goes to California
to live with her poet grandfather, they develop a
mutually beneficial relationship.

463. Ellis, Melvin Richard
THE WILD HORSE KILLERS   Gr. 6-10

Holt, 1976. O.P.; Scholastic paper $1.95.

Eighteen-year-old Sandra undertakes a fifteen-
day journey to save a band of wild horses from
airborne killers.

464. Epstein, Anne Merrick
GOOD STONES   Gr. 6-8

Houghton Mifflin, 1977. $6.95.

When her mother dies, Sisul Wabanaki, an
Abnaki Indian girl, flees from unpleasant relatives to a secluded mountain area, to make a
home for herself.

465. Evernden, Margery
THE DREAM KEEPER   Gr. 6-9

Lothrop, 1985. $10.25.

An old woman tells her great-granddaughter the
story of her journey from Poland and the trials

she endured as she made a new life for herself in America.

466. Evslin, Bernard
HERACLEA: A LEGEND OF WARRIOR WOMEN   Gr. 8-10

Macmillan/Four Winds, 1978. O.P.

A gutsy, vibrant variation of the myth of Hercules. Heraclea is a powerful nine-foot woman who becomes a goddess after performing formidable tasks.

467. Fitzhugh, Louise
NOBODY'S FAMILY IS GOING TO CHANGE   Gr. 6-8

Farrar, Straus & Giroux, 1974. $10.95; Dell paper $1.50. Gollancz (London), £4.95; Armada paper £1.25.

Emma wants to be a lawyer like her father; her brother Willie wants to be a dancer. Both face their father's displeasure. This is a penetrating story about family love lost. Emma comes to realize that she will never please her father and must pursue her own goals.

468. Flynn, Charlotte
DANGEROUS BEAT   Gr. 7-10

Pocket/Archway, 1985. $2.25 paper.

Jennifer Taggert lands a job as a copyperson/gofer at a local newspaper. When certain sensitive files begin to disappear, Jennifer finds herself in the middle of a mystery.

469. Forbes, Tom H.
QUINCY'S HARVEST   Gr. 6-8

Lippincott, 1976; dist. by Harper, $9.57.

Matters of life, death, and survival are contemplated by Quincy Evans, a sharecropper's son, who is increasingly disturbed by the hunting he does, even though he knows that nature's way is for some creatures to die so that others may live.

470. Forman, James
A FINE SOFT DAY   Gr. 7-12

Farrar, Straus & Giroux, 1978. O.P.

Brian O'Brien, middle brother in a Belfast Catholic family, is a good-hearted, peace-loving youth. When Brian's older brother dies, the ensuing violence brings Brian himself to the brink of desperation. This is a powerful and painful commentary on the bitter harvest of hatred.

471. Francis, Dorothy Brenner
CAPTAIN MORGANA MASON   Gr. 6-8

Dutton/Lodestar, 1982. O.P.

Morgana and her brother try to keep up their grandfather's sponge-diving operation in order to avoid living with their mother. Though their enterprise fails, they learn much about their mother and about family relationships.

472. Galbraith, Kathryn Osebold
COME SPRING   Gr. 6-9

Atheneum, 1979. $8.95.

When Reenie's family settles into a real house, Reenie becomes so anxious to maintain the family's roots that she fights against her father's attempt to move them again in the spring.

473. Garcia, Ann O'Neal
SPIRIT ON THE WALL   Gr. 8-9

Holiday House, 1982. $9.95.

> Handicapped Em would have been killed by her
> Cro-Magnon tribe if her grandmother had not
> saved her. Em, an artist, sets out with her brother
> and grandmother, to carve an independent life.

474. Garrigue, Sheila
THE ETERNAL SPRING OF MR. ITO   Gr. 6-9

Bradbury, 1985; dist. by Macmillan, $11.95.

> In British Columbia at the start of World War II,
> Sara, a British war evacuee who lives with her
> uncle's family, watches with dismay as anti-
> Japanese feeling grows and her friends the Itos
> are sent to an internment camp.

475. Girion, Barbara
A TANGLE OF ROOTS   Gr. 7-12

Scribner, 1979. $9.95.

> Sixteen-year-old Beth Frankle and her father
> must adapt to life after the sudden death of
> Beth's mother from a cerebral hemorrhage. A
> poignant, sensitive story.

476. Greene, Bette
SUMMER OF MY GERMAN SOLDIER   Gr. 6-9

Dial, 1973. $9.95.
Puffin paper (London), £1.25.

> In Arkansas during World War II, a lonely Jewish
> girl decides to help a German prisoner of war
> who has been kind and respectful to her.

477. Guernsey, JoAnn Bren
JOURNEY TO ALMOST THERE   Gr. 7-9

Clarion, 1985; dist. by Ticknor & Fields, $11.95.

> Because she is angry at her mother, Alison O'Brien sets out on a cross country drive with her grandfather to visit and perhaps to live with the father who abandoned her as a baby. Along the way Grandfather reminisces about his daughter-in-law when she was a young, single mother, giving Alison new insights into her mother's behavior.

478. Hall, Lynn
DANZA!   Gr. 6-7

Scribner, 1981. $11.95.

> Paulo, a quiet, sensitive Puerto Rican boy, feels the odd one out in his family and unable to live up to the masculine ideal set by his older brother. He does enjoy working with his grandfather's prize-winning Paso Fino horses, however, and becomes especially attached to one of them, a colt named Danza. When Danza must travel to the U.S. for special medical treatment, Paulo accompanies him and develops a satisfying sense of his own independence and abilities.

479. _____

FLOWERS OF ANGER   Gr. 7-9

Avon paper, 1976. $1.95.

> Carey is upset when her best friend Ann insists upon going through with plans for revenge against the neighbor who shot and killed Ann's straying horse.

480. _____

JUST ONE FRIEND   Gr. 6-10

Scribner, 1985. $11.95.

> Dory is a mentally slow girl who is terror-stricken at the thought of entering high school after having had three years of special education. She shows an inspiring determination to succeed in spite of many obstacles.

481. _____

TIN CAN TUCKER   Gr. 6-12

Scribner, 1982. $10.95.

> After running away from an unhappy situation in a home for kids, Ann Tucker heads for the rodeo, where she becomes a champion.

482. Hamilton, Virginia
ARILLA SUNDOWN   Gr. 7-10

Greenwillow, 1976. $12.50.

> Twelve year old Arilla, a black girl, is uncertain about her place in her family and her relationship with her brother. In the end though, she finds security in her decision to become a writer.

483. _____

A LITTLE LOVE   Gr. 8-12

Putnam/Philomel, 1984. $10.95.

> A black high school girl is helped through her rite of passage by a confrontation with her father and by her supportive boyfriend.

484. _____

    M.C. HIGGINS, THE GREAT   Gr. 7-10

    Macmillan, 1974. $10.95.

> Winner of the Newbery award, this is the coming-of-age story of a memorable black character, M.C. Higgins, who worries about a strip mining heap whose pollution threatens his family's home.

485. _____

    SWEET WHISPERS, BROTHER RUSH   Gr. 7-10

    Putnam/Philomel, 1982. $10.95.

> In this emotional story about a family in crisis, Tree, the young black narrator, goes back in time to explore not only her childhood, when she was abused by her mother, but her mother's childhood as well.

486. Hanson, June Andrea
    SUMMER OF THE STALLION   Gr. 6-9

    Macmillan, 1979. $9.95.

> Janey is proud of her ability to accomplish whatever her grandfather expects her to do. But when she tries to help him track down a wild stallion, she finds her sympathies for the animal causing a conflict.

487. Hautzig, Deborah
    HEY, DOLLFACE   Gr. 7-10

    Morrow, 1978. $11.88.

> The question of sexual identities is addressed when two fifteen-year-old girls must confront their feelings about each other. There are no explicit scenes and the relationship is not consummated. This will answer questions many teens have about same-sex feelings.

488. Hewitt, Marsha and Mackay, Claire
    ONE PROUD SUMMER   Gr. 6-9

    Women's Press, 1981. $6.95 paper.

    > A thirteen-year-old mill worker tells the story of a
    > strike against Montreal Cottons in which, in 1946,
    > she, her mother, and her grandmother took part.

489. Hickman, Janet
    THE STONES   Gr. 6-8

    Macmillan, 1976. $9.95.

    > During World War II, young Garrett McKay be-
    > comes involved with some boys who are harass-
    > ing an elderly recluse because of the man's
    > German surname. Their actions lead to the
    > man's losing his home and his independence.
    > Garrett is forced to realize that misguided pa-
    > triotism is both meaningless and destructive.

490. Highwater, Jamake
    LEGEND DAYS   Gr. 8-10

    Harper & Row, 1984. $10.89.

    > This first book in a projected three-part series,
    > describes the bitter experiences of the Plains In-
    > dians as seen through the eyes of ten-year-old
    > Amana. In a vision she is told to dress as a male.
    > When the gods instruct her to go back to her nor-
    > mal life the next year, Amana has a hard time
    > forgetting the power and adventure she experi-
    > enced when disguised as a man.

491. Hilgartner, Beth
    A NECKLACE OF FALLEN STARS   Gr. 6-8

    Little, Brown, 1979. $8.95.

    > The willful princess Kaela runs away when her
    > father tries to marry her off to a ruthless duke.

She meets a minstrel and they earn a living with his music and her storytelling. Gradually they fall in love. But their happiness is threatened because Kaela's father has sent an evil wizard after her to bring her back.

492. Hinton, S.E.
     TEX   Gr. 7-9

     Delacorte, 1979. $10.95; Dell paper $2.50.
     Gollancz (London), £4.95; Fontana paper £1.00.

     Set in the American Southwest, this is the story of two teenage brothers who must fend for themselves. It presents an especially effective picture of a boy who grows to responsible young adulthood as he sorts out his feelings about his absent father and his older brother whom he both loves and resents.

493. Holland, Isabelle
     OF LOVE, DEATH, AND OTHER JOURNEYS   Gr. 7-10

     Lippincott, 1975. $12.02.
     Published as *Ask No Questions* by Macdonald and Jane's, O.P.

     Although Meg's affectionate family live an easy, happy life in Italy, Meg wonders about her real father, whom she has never met. Then she learns her mother is dying—and that her father is coming to visit.

494. Hoover, H.M.
     THE DELIKON   Gr. 6-9

     Viking, 1977. $9.95.

     In this well-wrought science fiction novel, a number of philosophical questions are examined. An alien named Varina is caught between allegiances when her people, who had conquered Earth years before, are challenged by Earthling rebels.

495. Hughes, Monica
    ISIS PEDLAR   Gr. 6-10

    Atheneum, 1983. $9.95.

    Fifteen-year-old Moira must leave her planet, Isis, and go to Earth where her ne'er-do-well father is causing all sorts of problems.

496. Hunt, Irene
    WILLIAM   Gr. 6-9

    Scribner, 1977. $11.95; Ace paper $2.25.

    Although Mama is dying, she struggles to make a home for her children. When Sarah, a pregnant runaway teenager, moves in next door, she and Mama help each other, and their two families blend into one strong enough to hold together after Mama's death.

497. Hunter, Mollie
    THE THIRD EYE   Gr. 6-9

    Harper & Row, 1979. $11.49.
    Hamish Hamilton (London), £4.75.

    In Scotland in the 1930s, fourteen-year-old Jinty Morrison finds herself in a moral dilemma—should she reveal that the death of the Earl of Ballinford was a suicide? A sub-plot involves Jinty's strong-willed mother, who wants her daughters to attend university, and Jinty's two sisters, each determined to follow her own way.

498. Hurmence, Belinda
    A GIRL CALLED BOY   Gr. 6-8

    Clarion, 1982; dist. by Ticknor & Fields, $9.95.

> Boy, a young black girl, is tired of hearing about slavery days. But when she is thrust back in time, she learns firsthand about the suffering, both physical and psychological, of the slave.

499. _____

    TOUGH TIFFANY   Gr. 6-8

    Doubleday, 1980. $9.95.

> Tiffany Cox, an eleven-year-old black girl, tries to strike a balance between her strict grandmother and her disorganized, somewhat irresponsible mother.

500. Irwin, Hadley
    WHAT ABOUT GRANDMA?   Gr. 6-9

    Atheneum, 1982. $9.95.

> A grandmother, mother and daughter strengthen their relationships with each other while they close the grandmother's house before she enters a nursing home. A warm, sensitive story.

501. Johnson, Dorothy M.
    BUFFALO WOMAN   Gr. 6-9

    Dodd Mead, 1977. O.P.

> A Sioux woman named Whirlwind is the focus in this detailed picture of Sioux life and culture.

502. Johnston, Norma
    GABRIEL'S GIRL   Gr. 7-12

    Atheneum, 1983. $12.95.

> Seventeen-year-old Sarah flies to Spain to visit

her diplomat father only to learn he has vanished. Her desire to find him leads her into a web of international intrigue.

503. _____

THE KEEPING DAYS   Gr. 7-12
1973. Ace Paper $2.50.

GLORY IN THE FLOWER
1974. Ace paper $2.50.

THE SANCTUARY TREE
Atheneum, 1977. $7.95.

A MUSTARD SEED OF MAGIC
Atheneum, 1977. $8.95.

Tish Sterling, who is fourteen years old in the first book, narrates her family's experiences as well as the changes she is going through. She wants to be a writer and pursues her goal with determination.

504. Kennedy, Stephanie
HEY, DIDI DARLING   Gr. 6-8

Houghton Mifflin, 1983. $9.95.

A group of girls in a rock band think they're not getting gigs because of their sex, so they come up with a unique idea to promote themselves.

505. Kennemore, Tim
CHANGING TIMES   Gr. 8-12

Faber & Faber, 1984. $14.95.

Fifteen-year-old Victoria is able to travel backward and forward in time. What she learns on these journeys helps her to take control of her life.

506. Kerr, M.E.
     DINKY HOCKER SHOOTS SMACK   Gr. 7-10

     Harper & Row, 1972. $10.89.
     Heineman Education (London), £.75.

           Dinky Hocker is unhappy but cannot get her par-
           ents' attention—they're too busy doing social
           work with drug addicts. A lively comedy with a
           serious underlying message.

507. Klein, Norma
     THE CHEERLEADER   Gr. 7-9

     Knopf, 1985. $11.95.

           Sensitive Evan Siegal decides that boys should
           become cheerleaders for the girls' teams.

508. Knudson, R.R.
     RINEHART LIFTS   Gr. 5-7

     Farrar, Straus & Giroux, 1980. $9.95;
     Avon paper $1.95.

           Peace-loving Rinehart learns to lift weights
           under the tutelage of athletic Zan (Suzanne)
           Hagen.

509. _____

     ZAN HAGEN'S MARATHON   Gr. 8-10

     Farrar, Straus & Giroux, 1984. $10.95.

           Suzanne "Zan" Hagen, athlete extraordinaire,
           the heroine of a series of sports stories, gets her
           chance to run in the Olympics.

510. Lasky, Kathryn
     BEYOND THE DIVIDE   Gr. 6-10

     Macmillan, 1983. $11.95.

           An Amish girl and her father go west in the

nineteenth century and suffer deprivations on the trail.

511. L'Engle, Madeline
RING OF ENDLESS LIGHT   Gr. 7-10

Farrar, Straus & Giroux, 1980. $10.95; Dell paper $2.95.

> Sixteen-year-old Vicki Austin must cope with moving, her grandmother's imminent death, and the death of a friend. In this emotional time, the support of some special people and her own strength help Vicki overcome her grief.

512. Lingard, Joan
THE CLEARANCE   Gr. 7-10
Hamish Hamilton (London), 1974. £5.50.

THE RESETTLING
Hamish Hamilton (London), 1975. £5.50.

THE PILGRIMAGE
Hamish Hamilton (London), 1977. £4.25.

THE REUNION
Hamish Hamilton (London), 1977. £5.95.

> A forthright Scottish working-class girl named Maggie McKinley must struggle for things many girls take for granted. Her family does not want to help her get an education and the middle-class family of a boy she likes disapprove of her. In the final books, Maggie's perseverance makes her wish for an education come true.

513. Lively, Penelope
THE HOUSE IN NORHAM GARDENS   Gr. 6-9

Dutton, 1974. $8.95.
Heineman (London), £3.95.

> Fantasy and reality are blended in this challenging story of an English girl named Clare, who lives in a large old house with two great-aunts

who were liberated women before liberation was
fashionable.

514. Lord, Athena
A SPIRIT TO RIDE THE WILD WIND   Gr. 6-8

Macmillan, 1981. $10.95.

In Lowell, Massachusetts in 1836, twelve-year-
old Binnie Howe learns firsthand about the hardships of a millworker's life.

515. Lowry, Lois
A SUMMER TO DIE   Gr. 7-9

Houghton Mifflin, 1979. $10.95; Bantam paper $2.25.

Meg tells the story of her sister's death from
leukemia—which also helps Meg to mature and
the whole family to grow closer in their grief.

516. MacLeod, Charlotte
WE DARE NOT GO A-HUNTING   Gr. 6-8

Atheneum, 1980. $8.95.

Forthright and determined Molly Bassett solves
the mystery of what happened to Annette South-
erby, who had been kidnapped the previous year
from her parents' summer house on Netaquid Island.

517. McKinley, Robin
BEAUTY   Gr. 7-10

Harper & Row, 1979. $9.89.

An interesting retelling of *Beauty and the Beast*
in which Beauty saves the lives of both her father
and the Beast.

518. _____

    THE HERO AND THE CROWN   Gr. 6-10

    Greenwillow, 1984. $11.00.

        In a mythical kingdom, Aerin goes on a quest for her birthright, and becomes first a dragon killer and then the savior of her country.

519. Madison, Winifred
    CALL ME DANICA   Gr. 6-8

    Macmillan/Four Winds, 1977. O.P.

        When her father dies, Danica and her family emigrate from Croatia to Vancouver, where they struggle to adjust and begin a new life.

520. _____

    THE GENESSEE QUEEN   Gr. 7-9

    Delacorte, 1977. O.P.

        Monica thinks she would rather live with her violinist father than with her mother who is divorced from him, but when he comes to visit she begins to see both his weaknesses and her mother's good qualities.

521. Magnuson, James and Petrie, Dorothea G.
    ORPHAN TRAIN   Gr. 9-12

    Dial, 1978. O.P.

        Emma, unmarried at twenty-eight, finds herself in charge of a train full of New York City orphans bound for homes in the West, in the mid-nineteenth century.

522. Mahey, Margaret
    THE CHANGEOVER: A SUPERNATURAL　　　Gr. 8-10
    ROMANCE

    Atheneum, 1984. $11.95.

    > Carmody Braque, a demon who saps the strength of his victims, is preying on Laura's younger brother and the teen-aged girl must unleash her own supernatural powers to save him.

523. Mark, Jan
    HANDLES　　　　　　　　　　　　　　　　Gr. 6-8

    Atheneum, 1985. $12.95.

    > Sent to spend part of her summer vacation with stodgy, dull relatives in the country, Erica finds refuge with Elsie, the male proprietor of a motorcycle repair shop, with whom she can share her love of cycles.

524. Mathis, Sharon Bell
    LISTEN FOR THE FIG TREE　　　　　　　　Gr. 7-9

    Viking, 1974. $9.95.

    > Muffin Johnson struggles to keep her life together in a depressing environment. Supportive friends help her regain her interest in life after she is raped. There is a great deal of warmth and love in this sensitive young black girl's story.

525. Mazer, Harry
    THE ISLAND KEEPER　　　　　　　　　　　Gr. 7-12

    Delacorte, 1981. $8.95; Dell paper $2.50.

    > A runaway girl whose mother and sister have died finds her way to an uninhabited Canadian lake island owned by her wealthy father. There, as she successfully copes with survival, she

develops a satisfying sense of self-confidence and self-reliance.

526. _____

THE WAR ON VILLA STREET   Gr. 6-9

Delacorte, 1978. O.P.; Dell paper $2.50.

Willis Pier has an alcoholic father and he is threatened by a predatory gang of toughs. He must work through these problems and develop self-respect on which he can rely for the rest of his life.

527. _____

WHEN THE PHONE RANG   Gr. 8-12

Scholastic, 1985. $11.95.

When their parents are killed in a plane crash, two teenaged boys try to make a home for their twelve-year-old sister.

528. Mazer, Norma Fox
UP IN SETH'S ROOM   Gr. 7-12

Delacorte, 1979. $7.95; Dell paper $2.50.

Fifteen-year-old Finn Rousseau has decided to remain a virgin although her friends and her older sister do not accept her attitude for themselves. When Finn meets Seth, however, a relationship develops that causes both of them to reevaluate their attitudes toward sex.

529. Meyer, Carolyn
THE LUCK OF TEXAS MC COY   Gr. 8-12

Atheneum, 1984. $11.95.

Sixteen-year-old Texas McCoy is determined to make a success of the run-down New Mexico ranch she has inherited from her father. While she works toward her goal she has to learn that everybody needs friends.

530. _____

THE SUMMER I LEARNED ABOUT LIFE   Gr. 7-9

Atheneum, 1983. $11.95.

It is 1928 and fifteen-year-old Teddie wants to be an aviatrix. Her family doesn't think it's a suitable career for a girl, who should be planning for marriage and a family. But Teddie knows she will fly someday.

531. Miles, Betty
THE TROUBLE WITH THIRTEEN   Gr. 6-8

Knopf, 1979. $6.99; Camelot/Avon $2.25.

Friendship is at the heart of this story about Annie Morrison, who is not ready to grow up. She finds comfort in a special relationship with a sympathetic friend.

532. Miller, Sandy
CHASE THE SUN   Gr. 7-10

NAL/Signet/Vista paper, 1983. O.P.

In this teen romance, a high school student pilot is determined to earn both her flying license and her instructor's affection.

533. Mills, Claudia
WHAT ABOUT ANNIE?   Gr. 6-9

Walker, 1985. $9.95.

The realistic story of thirteen-year-old Annie Bodansky, who tries to keep her family together when her father loses his job during the Depression.

534. Moeri, Louise
     FIRST THE EGG   Gr. 6-12

     Dutton, 1982. $10.95; Archway paper $1.75.

          Male and female students pair up in a high school
          class on marriage and the family; each couple is
          given an egg to care for as though it were a baby.
          The object is to give each couple an idea of what
          parenthood is like.

535. Monjo, F.N.
     THE PORCELAIN PAGODA   Gr. 6-8

     Viking, 1976. O.P.

          Kitty McAllister's experiences aboard her
          father's merchant ship provide an interesting pic-
          ture of the China trade in the nineteenth century.

536. Myers, Walter Dean
     THE YOUNG LANDLORDS   Gr. 6-9

     Viking, 1979. $11.50.

          Five friends who live in New York City are startled
          to find themselves the owners of an aged apart-
          ment building when the landlord unloads it for
          $1.00. Although the boys and girls work hard to
          try to make a go of the project, they find out that
          landlording isn't as easy as it seems. A funny
          story with serious undertones.

537. Newton, Suzanne
     AN END TO PERFECT   Gr. 6-8

     Viking, 1984. $11.50.

          Arden learns the hard way that to keep troubled
          DorJo's friendship she must give DorJo room to
          decide whether or not to return to her irresponsi-
          ble mother.

538. _____

    M.V. SEXTON SPEAKING   Gr. 7-11

    Viking, 1981. $9.95; Fawcett paper $2.25.

        Down-to-earth Martha Sexton gets a summer job at a bakery and discovers that as she gains financial independence a better relationship develops between her and her guardian aunt and uncle.

539. O'Brien, Robert C.
    Z FOR ZACHARIAH   Gr. 7-10

    Atheneum, 1975. $10.95.

        Ann Burden's diary tells a tale of the aftermath of almost total destruction. Ann believes she is the only living person on the planet, until she runs into a masked male stranger. Dramatic science fiction.

540. O'Dell, Scott
    CARLOTA   Gr. 6-8

    Houghton Mifflin, 1977. $10.95.

        Carlota de Zubaran is a sixteen-year-old girl in nineteenth-century California. She has been raised by her father to take the place of the son he lost in an Indian raid.

541. O'Neal, Zibby
    IN SUMMER LIGHT   Gr. 9-12

    Viking/Kestrel, 1985. $11.95.

        A seventeen-year-old artist spends the summer with her father, from whom she has been estranged. Kate learns to look beyond her father's pomposity and self-absorption and to accept him despite these flaws.

542. Park, Ruth
PLAYING BEATIE BOW   Gr. 6-9

Atheneum, 1982. $12.95; Penguin paper $3.50.

A haunting fantasy in which a fourteen-year-old
Australian girl finds herself in Sydney in Victorian
times. She must call up all her strength and intel-
lect to cope with this chilling situation.

543 Paterson, Katherine
COME SING, JIMMY JO   Gr. 6-10

Dutton, 1985. $12.50.

This is a poignant, sensitive story about an Ap-
palachian boy who overcomes his shyness
about his singing talent and in the process also
learns that it takes a lot of love to hold a family
together.

544. _____

JACOB HAVE I LOVED   Gr. 6-9

Harper/Crowell, 1980. $10.95; Avon paper $2.50.
Gollancz (London), £5.95; Puffin paper £1.75.

Louise, bitter at living in the shadow of her fa-
vored and musically talented twin sister, must
leave her Chesapeake Bay island home to seek
out her own identity and gain a sense of worth.

545. Peck, Richard
ARE YOU IN THE HOUSE ALONE?   Gr. 7-12

Viking, 1976. $11.50.

After a high school girl is raped she is confronted
with an unsympathetic system of justice. It is true
that official attitudes have changed since this
book was first published but it works as a troub-
ling exposition of what used to be and too often
still is.

153

546. _____

THE GHOST BELONGED TO ME   Gr. 6-9
Viking, 1975. $10.95; Dell paper $2.25.

GHOSTS I HAVE BEEN
Viking, 1977. $11.50; Dell paper $2.50.

THE DREADFUL FUTURE OF BLOSSOM CULP
Delacorte, 1983. $13.95; Dell paper $2.50.

Action, comedy, and a good dose of the supernatural fuel these intriguing stories about the
forthright Blossom Culp, whose psychic abilities
bring her more than her share of adventure.

547. _____

REPRESENTING SUPERDOLL   Gr. 7-9

Viking, 1974. O.P.

When Verna tries to help her friend Darlene win
some beauty contests, she comes to realize that
beauty is more than regular features and a nice
smile.

548. Peterson, P.J.
NOBODY ELSE CAN WALK IT FOR YOU   Gr. 7-10

Delacorte, 1982. O.P.

Eighteen-year-old Laura leads a coed "Y" group
on a camp-out. The group encounters real
danger, when they are threatened by three
motorcyclists.

549. Pevsner, Stella
CUTE IS A FOUR LETTER WORD   Gr. 6-8

Houghton/Clarion, 1980. $10.50; Archway paper $1.95.

This is the comic story—with a good deal of substance beneath its humorous surface—of a
pivotal year in the life of Clara, a junior high
school student who finds that some of her goals
may not be as important as she had believed.

550. Peyton, K.M.
THE TEAM   Gr. 6-9

Harper/Crowell; Oxford University Press (London), 1976. O.P.

> Headstrong Ruth Hollis works at improving her riding skills and conquering her fears of cross-country racing so that she might become a credible Pony Club team member; meanwhile, her new pony is the cause of a strained relationship with her friend Peter.

551. Pfeffer, Susan Beth
A MATTER OF PRINCIPLE   Gr. 7-10

Delacorte, 1982. $9.95; Dell paper $2.25.

> When Becca is prohibited from publishing an article in her high school paper that is critical of the school, she and her friends start an underground newspaper of their own.

552. Phipson, Joan
FLY INTO DANGER   Gr. 6-8

Atheneum, 1977. $6.95.
Methuen (London), O.P.

> Margaret's visit to London to see her mother, an opera singer, takes on an unexpected element of adventure when she crosses paths with a pair of bird poachers.

553. Piekarski, Vicki, ed.
WESTWARD THE WOMEN   Gr. 9-12

Doubleday, 1984. $11.95.

> An anthology of twelve Western stories written by women like Willa Cather, Mari Sandoz, and Dorothea M. Johnson.

554. Price, Susan
    FROM WHERE I STAND   Gr. 10-12

    Faber & Faber, 1984. $11.95.

    > Seventeen-year-old Kama is called "Paki" and "Wog" by her classmates. She vents her anger and frustration by exposing the mindless prejudice of the other students.

555. Quinn-Harkin, Janet
    LOVE MATCH   Gr. 7-10

    Bantam (Sweet Dreams), 1982. O.P.

    > The tomboy daughter of athletic parents must decide if she should hone her tennis skills when she meets up with an attractive male teammate. She's afraid, at first, that he won't like her to play as well as or better than he does but she realizes she has to do her best.

556. Raskin, Ellen
    THE WESTING GAME   Gr. 6-8

    Dutton, 1978. $11.00; Avon paper $2.25.
    Macmillan (London), O.P.

    > A witty, superbly crafted mystery in which sixteen players participate in multimillionaire industrialist Sam Westing's mysterious, challenging game which is designed to find out who among them is worthy to be his heir. A young girl outsmarts them all.

557. Ray, Mary
    THE WINDOWS OF ELISSA   Gr. 6-9

    Faber & Faber, 1982. $11.95.

    > Carthage in the third century B.C. is the setting for this story of Elissa and her sister, Sophie, who

> must stay behind the city's strong walls for three years while Carthage is besieged by Syracuse.

558. Riordan, James
THE WOMAN IN THE MOON AND OTHER   Gr. 5-9
TALES OF FORGOTTEN HEROINES

Dial, 1985. $11.95.

> This is an excellent collection of stories from around the world with independent, clever heroines. A useful bibliography is appended.

559. Rockwood, Joyce
TO SPOIL THE SUN   Gr. 7-10

Holt, Rinehart & Winston, 1976. O.P.

> A memorable novel about a young Cherokee woman whose life is permeated by tragedy as her people suffer the effects of invasion by the white man.

560. Rodgers, Raboo
MAGNUM FAULT   Gr. 7-9

Houghton Mifflin, 1984. $10.95.

> Two teenagers foil a gas company's environmentally catastrophic scheme to shore up its dwindling reserves. The heroine is a larger-than-life character who is able to take care of herself. Suspenseful.

561. Rodowsky, Colby
JULIE'S DAUGHTER   Gr. 8-10

Farrar, Straus, & Giroux, 1985. $11.95.

> A novel with three strong women characters: seventeen-year-old Mary Rose; her mother Julie, who was seventeen when she left Mary Rose to be raised by her own mother; and a fierce old art-

ist, Harper Teggs. The recently reunited Julie and Mary Rose forge their relationship as they care for the terminally ill Teggs, who is determined to die at home.

562. St. George, Judith
IN THE SHADOW OF THE BEAR   Gr. 7-10

Putnam, 1984. $10.95.

Seventeen-year-old Annie dreads going camping with her father in the Arctic circle. Unexpected events prove that she is stronger than she had thought.

563. Sallis, Susan
ONLY LOVE   Gr. 9-12

Harper & Row, 1980. $11.06.

A terminally ill paraplegic teen manages to deal with tragedy through her own good humor, passion for life, and support from the boy who loves her. An exceptionally strong female character.

564. Schlee, Ann
ASK ME NO QUESTIONS   Gr. 6-9

Holt, Rinehart & Winston, 1982. $14.50.
Macmillan (London), £3.95.

In 1848, a sister and brother leave London to avoid a cholera epidemic. At their new home, when they discover that hundreds of children are being kept in abominable conditions in a nearby workhouse, they set out to help them.

565. Scott, Carol J.
KENTUCKY DAUGHTER   Gr. 7-10

Clarion, 1985. $12.95.

Mary Fred Pratley must leave her Kentucky hill

home to get a good education because she wants to become a teacher. She finds it difficult to adjust to a new environment but she is sustained by her pride in her family and her background.

566. Sebestyen, Ouida
IOU'S   Gr. 6-9

Atlantic Monthly Press, 1982; dist. by Little, Brown, $12.45.

There is a warm mother-son relationship in this story of a boy who must deal with the re-appearance of the grandfather who treated the boy's mother unkindly.

567. _____

WORDS BY HEART   Gr. 5-9

Atlantic Monthly Press, 1979; dist. by Little, Brown, $11.45; Bantam paper $2.25.

Prejudice generates tragedy in this powerful story of a black girl, Lena Sills, and her family, who left their all-black town of Scattercreek for hopes of a better life in the Oklahoma territory of the 1890s.

568. Singer, Isaac Beshevis
YENTL, THE YESHIVA BOY   Gr. 8-12

Farrar, Straus & Giroux, 1984. $10.95.

Handsome woodcuts illustrate this tale about an orphaned young Jewish woman who disguises herself as a man so that she can study the Torah.

569. Singer, Marilyn
THE HORSEMASTER   Gr. 7-9

Atheneum, 1985. $13.95.

A contemporary girl is thrust back in time to a

foreign land where she plays a key role in stabilizing a ruler's troubled kingdom.

570. Slepian, Jan
THE ALFRED SUMMER   Gr. 6-8

Macmillan, 1980. $8.95; Scholastic paper $1.95.

Lester has cerebral palsy, Alfred is retarded, Myron is repressed by his family, and Claire refuses to be pushed around. The four become unlikely friends in this story of major struggles and minor but significant triumphs.

571. _____

GETTING ON WITH IT   Gr. 7-9

Macmillan/Four Winds, 1985. $11.95.

When Berry is sent to visit her grandmother while her parents are getting a divorce, she meets several neighbors whose eventful lives give her a new perspective on her relationship with her parents and on their divorce.

572. Stanek, Lou Willet
MEGAN'S BEAT   Gr. 6-9

Dial, 1983. $10.95.

Although Megan is looking forward to high school, she fears that she will have trouble getting into the thick of things because she is a farm kid. However, she becomes very popular and manages to get the farm and city kids together in the bargain.

573. Stone, Bruce
HALF NELSON, FULL NELSON   Gr. 7-11

Harper & Row, 1985. $12.50.

In this satirical novel, sixteen-year-old Nelson Gato becomes the loving, nurturing center for his family while his father pursues his dream of becoming a big-time wrestler.

574. Stone, Josephine Rector
GREEN IS FOR GALANX   Gr. 6-9

Atheneum, 1980. O.P.

Seventeen-year-old Illona is in charge of exceptionally brilliant children. She saves them from scientists who plan to experiment with their minds.

575. Strauss, Victoria
WORLDSTONE   Gr. 7-12

Macmillan/Four Winds, 1985. $13.95.

In this fantasy a girl is drawn by her strong, untrained telepathic powers into a struggle between two warring factions in an alternative world. Through her involvement, she gains maturity and control over her powers.

576. Streiber, Whitley
WOLF OF SHADOWS   Gr. 6-8

Knopf, 1985. $9.95.

A girl and her mother, an ethologist studying wolves in a remote wilderness area, survive a nuclear attack. As nuclear winter sets in, the two bond with the wolf pack for mutual support and make their way south to a warmer climate where chances are better for continued survival.

577. Sutton, Larry
TAILDRAGGERS HIGH   Gr. 6-8

Farrar, Straus & Giroux, 1985. $11.95.

Twelve-year-old Jessie Oates has flying in her blood, but her grandfather and her mother try to discourage her from becoming a pilot; her father was a flyer who was killed in Vietnam.

578. Szabo, Joseph
ALMOST GROWN   Gr. 7-12

Crown/Harmony, 1978. O.P.

Photographs of teens along with poems culled from a poetry workshop create a sensitive, intimate picture of adolescence.

579. Taylor, Janet Lisle
SIRENS AND SPIES   Gr. 6-9

Bradbury, 1985. $11.95.

Both Elsie and her older sister learn a painful lesson about friendship when they discover their idolized piano teacher's past. The teacher, a French emigré, was a collaborator during World War II. As the girls struggle to accept this disturbing fact, their ideas about loyalties are challenged.

580. Taylor, Mildred
SONG OF THE TREES   Gr. 6-10
Dial, 1975. $7.95.

ROLL OF THE THUNDER, HEAR MY CRY
Dial, 1976. $12.95.
Gollancz (London), £6.50.

LET THE CIRCLE BE UNBROKEN
Dial, 1981. $14.95; Bantam paper $2.95.
Gollancz (London), £6.50; Puffin paper £1.95.

In this trio of novels, set during the Depression, the black Logan family struggle to hold on to their Mississippi farm. Narrator Cassie Logan's voice is striking, if sometimes a little too wise for her years. *Roll of Thunder, Hear My Cry* won the Newbery award.

581. Thomas, Joyce Carol
     CHILDREN OF THE SUN   Gr. 6-8

     Zamani Productions, 1981. O.P.

> Tom Feelings's deft, sombre portraits of black children are paired with poet Thomas's expressive evocation of childhood: "Shall I draw a magic landscape?/In the genius of my fingers/I hold the seeds/Can I grow a painting like a flower?/Can I sculpture a future without weeds?" (Stapled.)

582. _____

     MARKED BY FIRE   Gr. 8-12

     Avon/Flare, 1982. $2.25 paper.

> Abbysinia Jackson suffers the trauma of rape. But the black women of her small Oklahoma town are so supportive that she regains her equilibrium. A powerful, moving novel.

583. Thrasher, Crystal
     THE DARK DIDN'T CATCH ME   Gr. 7-10
     Aladin paper, 1975. $1.95.

     BETWEEN DARK AND DAYLIGHT
     Atheneum, 1979. $10.95.

     JULIE'S SUMMER
     Atheneum, 1981. $12.95.

     END OF A DARK ROAD
     Atheneum, 1982. $12.95.

     A TASTE OF DAYLIGHT
     Atheneum, 1984. $12.95.

> This is a saga of the life of Seely, a teenager, and her family during the Depression of the 1930s. They move from the country to the city and then back again, searching for some kind of financial security.

584. Tolan, Stephanie S.
THE GREAT SKINNER STRIKE   Gr. 6-9

Macmillan, 1983. $8.95.

A working mother goes on strike when her family refuses to help her. When fourteen-year-old Jenny takes over the housework, she realizes her mother has a justified complaint.

585. _____

THE LIBERATION OF TANSY WARNER   Gr. 6-9

Scribner, 1980. $9.95.

Tansy Warner, fourteen years old, is the odd one out in her family; and the only one who understands the reasons why her mother has deserted them. This understanding helps to strengthen Tansy's character.

586. Towne, Mary
FIRST SERVE   Gr. 6-9

Atheneum, 1976. O.P.

Dulcie's parents have made plans for the future of Dulcie and her sister. But the plans are based on basically sexist thinking that must be revised when Dulcie's talent for tennis becomes too impressive to be ignored.

587. Turnbull, Ann
MAROO OF THE WINTER CAVES   Gr. 6-8

Clarion, 1984; dist. by Ticknor & Fields, $10.95.

In prehistoric times, Maroo, a young girl, undertakes a dangerous, lonely journey to get help for her family who are stranded without food to last through the winter.

588. Uchida, Yoshiko
A JAR OF DREAMS   Gr. 6-8
Atheneum, 1981. $11.95.

THE BEST BAD THING
Atheneum, 1983. $9.95.

THE HAPPIEST ENDING
Atheneum, 1985. $10.95.

>Rinko is an eleven-year-old Japanese-American girl who values her close-knit family but wants to be like the rest of her white classmates. These three novels share themes of pride in Japanese culture and descriptions of anti-Japanese feeling in America during the late 1930s. In *A Jar of Dreams*, Rinko meets her lively aunt who is visiting from Japan; in *The Best Bad Thing* she helps a discouraged widow to keep her farm going; and in *The Happiest Ending* she comes to understand the reasons for an arranged marriage, although she wants the freedom to choose her own husband some day.

589. Voigt, Cynthia
HOMECOMING   Gr. 6-9
Atheneum, 1981. $13.95; Fawcett paper $2.25.
Collins (London), £6.95; £3.95 paper.

DICEY'S SONG
Atheneum, 1982. $10.95.

>These two books follow the fortunes of young Dicey Tillerman, who shepherds her brothers and sisters from Connecticut to Maryland in search of relatives to take them in. In *Dicey's Song*, we find Dicey and her siblings settled in at their Gram's house; Dicey must give up some of her control over the family, and must learn how to accept love.

FICTION

590. _____

JACKAROO   Gr. 8-10

Atheneum, 1985. $14.95.

> Set in a fictional kingdom, this is the story of six-teen-year-old Gwyn, an innkeeper's daughter, who helps the downtrodden local serfs by taking on the identity of Jackaroo, a masked hero whose legendary bravery has been an inspiration to the people during hard times.

591. Wain, John
LIZZIE'S FLOATING SHOP   Gr. 7-9

Bodley Head, 1984. $6.95.
Bodley Head paper (London), £3.50.

> Lizzie opens a small shop aboard her uncle's canal boat, in order to earn money to buy her brother a new violin.

592. Walsh, Jill Paton
A PARCEL OF PATTERNS   Gr. 7-9

Farrar, Straus & Giroux, 1983. $10.95.

> A young woman writes a chronicle of the disasters brought to a Puritan colony by the plague and the reactions of the people to those disasters.

593. Walter, Mildred Pitts
TROUBLE'S CHILD   Gr. 7-9

Lothrop, 1985. $10.25.

> Fourteen-year-old Martha lives in a black community on a remote Louisiana island. She is expected to marry young and become a midwife like her grandmother. But since Martha has other ideas she must make the painful decision to leave the island in order to get an education.

594. Westfall, Robert
    THE MACHINE GUNNERS   Gr. 6-9

    Morrow/Greenwillow, 1976. $11.88.

    > Tragedy ensues when a group of boys salvage a
    > machine gun, build a fortress, and wait to defend
    > themselves against the enemy. A trenchant tale
    > of war and children.

595. White, Ellen
    THE PRESIDENT'S DAUGHTER   Gr. 7-10
    Avon/Flare, 1984. $2.95.

    WHITE HOUSE AUTUMN
    Avon/Flare, 1985. $2.95.

    > The heroine of these two books is sixteen-year-
    > old Meg, whose mother becomes the first woman
    > president of the United States. Meg must learn to
    > cope with the excitement and lack of privacy that
    > go with her new position.

596. Wilder, Cherry
    PRINCESS OF THE CHAMELN   Gr. 9-12

    Atheneum, 1984. $14.95.

    > In this fantasy a young princess is forced to dis-
    > guise herself as a soldier to save her life after her
    > parents are assassinated.

597. Wilkinson, Brenda Scott
    LUDELL   Gr. 6-9
    Harper & Row, 1975. $10.89.

    LUDELL AND WILLIE
    Harper & Row, 1977. $10.89.

    LUDELL'S NEW YORK TIME
    Harper & Row, 1980. $10.83.

    > This trio of stories is about a black girl who moves

from her home in Georgia to New York City where her mother lives. *Ludell* deals with life in a black Southern community twenty years ago; in *Ludell and Willie* Ludell has a romance with her neighbor, Willie; and in the final book Ludell adjusts to life in New York—a far cry from Waycross, Georgia.

598. Yarbro, Chelsea Quinn
FOUR HORSES FOR TISHTRAY   Gr. 6-8

Harper & Row, 1985. $12.50.

A Roman slave girl does trick horseback riding to win enough money to pay for her family's freedom.

599. Yep, Laurence
CHILD OF THE OWL   Gr. 6-8

Harper & Row, 1977. $11.89.

Casey, living with her grandmother in Chinatown, works out her identity as a young Chinese-American woman.

600. _____

SEA GLASS   Gr. 6-8

Harper & Row, 1979. $11.89.

When his family moves, Craig Chin, a Chinese-American boy, has trouble adjusting to the new town. He makes friends with an elderly man and a Caucasian girl, and they help him overcome his homesickness.

601. Zindel, Bonnie and Paul
A STAR FOR THE LATE COMER   Gr. 7-10

Harper & Row, 1980. O.P.; Bantam paper $2.25.
Bodley Head (London), £4.50; Armada paper £1.25.

Seventeen-year-old Brooke Hillary has always

obeyed her mother's wishes; but when her mother dies, Brooke realizes she must decide what she herself really wants to do and carry on her life accordingly.

Seventh Grade through Twelfth Grade
NON-FICTION

Jacket illustration by Mary Azarian from SEAFARING WOMEN by Linda Grant DePauw. Copyright © 1982 by Linda Grant DePauw. Reprinted by permission of Houghton Mifflin Company.

NON-FICTION

602. Alderman, Clifford Lindsey
ANNIE OAKLEY AND THE WORLD OF HER TIME   Gr. 6-8

Macmillan, 1979. $10.95.

>The real life of the popular folk figure.

603. Bertock, Alan
GIRL GROUPS   Gr. 8-12

Delilah Books, 1982; dist. by Putnam, O.P.

>An overview of the female vocal groups of the 1960s which provides an important part of musical history.

604. Biddle, Marcia McKenna
LABOR: CONTRIBUTIONS OF WOMEN   Gr. 6-9

Dillon, 1979. $8.95.

>These five labor movement workers are Mother Jones, Mary Heaton Vorse, Frances Perkins, Addie Wyatt, and Delores Huerta.

605. Blume, Arlene
ANNAPURNA: A WOMAN'S PLACE   Gr. 9-12

Sierra Club, 1980. $8.95.

>The gripping account of a climb up Mount Annapurna by thirteen women in 1978.

606. Bober, Natalie
BREAKING TRADITION: THE STORY OF   Gr. 7-10
LOUISE NEVELSON

Atheneum, 1984. $12.95.

>An admiring portrait of the innovative artist.

607. Boutet de Monvel, Louis Maurice
     JOAN OF ARC   Gr. 7-12

     Viking, 1980. $14.95.

          A facsimile of a nineteenth-century biography.

608. Bowman, Kathleen
     NEW WOMEN IN ART & DANCE   Gr. 4-6

     NEW WOMEN IN ENTERTAINMENT

     NEW WOMEN IN MEDIA

     NEW WOMEN IN MEDICINE

     NEW WOMEN IN POLITICS

     NEW WOMEN IN SOCIAL SCIENCES

     Creative Educational Society, 1976. $8.95 each.

          Well-written profiles of successful women.

609. Brooks, Polly Schoyer
     QUEEN ELEANOR: INDEPENDENT SPIRIT   Gr. 6-9
     OF THE MEDIEVAL WORLD

     Lippincott, 1983; dist. by Harper, $9.57.

          A biography of Eleanor of Acquitaine, who
          reigned for a while over both England and France.

610. Carlson, Dale
     BOYS HAVE FEELINGS TOO: GROWING   Gr. 6-9
     UP MALE FOR BOYS

     Atheneum, 1980. $9.95.

          Good   suggestions   for   breaking   male
          stereotypes.

611. Collard, Alexandra
     TWO YOUNG DANCERS: THEIR WORLD   Gr. 6-12
     OF BALLET

     Messner, 1984. $10.29.

174
          A teenaged boy and girl describe in their own

words their gradual immersion into the highly competitive and demanding world of dance.

612. Cooper, Ilene
    SUSAN B. ANTHONY   Gr. 7-10

    Franklin Watts, 1984. $9.95.

    > A biography of the nineteenth-century suffragist who also worked in the Abolitionist movement.

613. Currimbhoy, Nayana
    INDIRA GANDHI   Gr. 7-12

    Franklin Watts, 1985. $9.90.

    > A candid biography of the charismatic woman who became prime minister of one of the world's most populous countries.

614. Daugherty, Lynn B.
    WHY ME? HELP FOR VICTIMS OF CHILD   Gr. 7-12
    SEXUAL ABUSE (EVEN IF THEY ARE ADULTS NOW)

    Mother Courage Press, 1984. $7.95.

    > Brief case histories and frank advice about how to cope with the psychological trauma of being sexually abused.

615. DePauw, Linda Grant
    FOUNDING MOTHERS: WOMEN OF AMERICA   Gr. 6-9
    IN THE REVOLUTIONARY ERA

    Houghton Mifflin, 1975. $12.95.

    > A vivid look at the place of women in eighteenth-century America along with descriptions of everyday life.

616. _____

SEAFARING WOMEN   Gr. 9-12

Houghton Mifflin, 1982. $10.95.

> Colorful, detailed accounts of women who, through chance, design, or coercion went to sea aboard privateers, warships, whalers, or merchant vessels to serve as helpmates, prostitutes, cooks, and in some rare cases, even captains.

617. Dunnahoo, Terry
BEFORE THE SUPREME COURT: THE   Gr. 6-8
STORY OF BELVA ANN LOCKWOOD

Hougton Mifflin, 1974. O.P.

> A biography of a nineteenth-century woman who fought prejudice to become a lawyer and eventually address the Supreme Court.

618. Eagen, Andrea Boroff
WHY AM I SO MISERABLE IF THESE   Gr. 9-12
ARE THE BEST YEARS OF MY LIFE?

Lippincott, 1976; dist. by Harper, $11.49; Avon paper $2.25.

> Advice to adolescent girls from a feminist on self-development and the relationship between the sexes. Sexual matters are an important part of the discussion; information is included on the reproductive system, birth control, and abortion. The underlying theme is that a young woman should make intelligent decisions for herself.

619. English, Betty Lou
YOU CAN'T BE TIMID WITH A TRUMPET   Gr. 5-8

Lothrop, 1980. $11.25.

> Men and women from famous orchestras talk about their music and the instruments they play.

620. Faber, Doris
     BELLA ABZUG   Gr. 6-8

     Lothrop, 1976. $11.25.

          A lively biography.

621. Facklam, Margery
     WILD ANIMALS, GENTLE WOMEN   Gr. 6-9

     Harcourt Brace Jovanovich, 1978. $5.95.

          These profiles of eleven women who have made
          important contributions to the study of wild animals
          include Jane Goodall, the expert on chimpan-
          zees, and Dian Fossey, who has done extensive
          studies of gorillas.

622. Fox, Mary Virginia
     WOMEN ASTRONAUTS: ABOARD THE SHUTTLE   Gr. 6-8

     Messner, 1984. $9.79.

          Astronaut Sally K. Ride leads off this introduction
          to NASA's women astronauts. Even though
          grave misfortune has hurt NASA and its pro-
          grams recently, women astronauts are an impor-
          tant part of the past and will be present again
          when NASA resumes its activities.

623. Frayne, Trent
     FAMOUS WOMEN TENNIS PLAYERS   Gr. 7-12

     Dodd Mead, 1979. O.P.

          Twelve tennis stars of today and yesterday, in-
          cluding Virginia Wade, Billie Jean King, and
          Helen Wills.

624. Freedman, Russell
CHILDREN OF THE WILD WEST   Gr. 5-8

Clarion, 1983; dist. by Ticknor & Fields, $12.95.

> Old photographs and a smooth text give a good idea of what it was really like to be a child in the days of the American frontier.

625. Fritz, Jean
THE DOUBLE LIFE OF POCAHONTAS   Gr. 6-8

Putnam, 1983. $9.95.

> This arresting book about the Indian princess includes information about her life in England as the wife of John Rolf.

626. Fusco, Patricia and Fusco, Marina
MARINA AND RUBY   Gr. 6-8

Morrow, 1977. O.P.

> With patience, care, and love, Marina Fusco develops her young foal Ruby into a handsome riding horse.

627. Gaeddert, Lou Ann Bigge
ALL IN ALL: A BIOGRAPHY   Gr. 7-9
OF GEORGE ELIOT

Dutton, 1976. O.P.

> A sympathetic treatment of the life of the Victorian writer whose real name was Mary Anne Evans, and who created controversy when, in her thirties, she set up housekeeping with George Henry Lewes, a married man.

628. Gleasner, Diana
BREAKTHROUGH: WOMEN IN WRITING   Gr. 10-12
Walker, 1980. $9.90.

BREAKTHROUGH: WOMEN IN SCIENCE
Walker, 1983. $12.95.

> *Women in Writing* includes profiles of such diverse writers as Judy Blume, Erma Bombeck, Erica Jong, and Phyllis Whitney. In *Women in Science*, Gleasner introduces a number of women, not widely known, who have done outstanding work in science and technology.

629. Gornick, Vivian
WOMEN IN SCIENCE   Gr. 10-12

Simon & Schuster, 1983. O.P.

> An enlightening look at the successes and problems experienced by women scientists.

630. Greenfield, Eloise and Little, Lessie Jones
CHILDTIMES: A THREE   Gr. 6-8
GENERATIONAL MEMOIR

Harper/Crowell, 1979. $10.89.

> Author and poet Eloise Greenfield gathers the recollections of her mother and grandmother and joins them with her own in this three-part memoir of growing up black in the twentieth century.

631. Haber, Louis
WOMEN PIONEERS OF SCIENCE   Gr. 6-9

Harcourt Brace Jovanovich, 1979. $12.95.

> Nuclear physics, biochemistry, and medicine are three of the fields represented in these profiles of important women scientists.

632. Haney, Lynn
    CHRIS EVERT, THE YOUNG CHAMPION   Gr. 6-9

    Putnam, 1977. O.P.

    > An interesting portrait of the tennis star.

633. Haskins, James
    KATHERINE DUNHAM   Gr. 6-8

    Coward-McCann, 1982. $10.95.

    > A biography of the dynamic black dancer and choreographer who was trained as an anthropologist and studied the cultural traditions of black dance in the West Indies.

634. _____

    LENA HORNE   Gr. 7-10

    Coward-McCann, 1983. $10.95.

    > A briskly written account of the singer from her birth in 1917 to her smash broadway hit, *Lena Horne: The Lady and Her Music*.

635. Hodgman, Ann and Djabbaroff, Ruby
    SKYSTARS: THE HISTORY OF   Gr. 7-12
    WOMEN IN AVIATION

    Atheneum, 1981. $11.95.

    > This book includes balloonists, parachutists, and stunt flyers, as well as military pilots and the members of the space shuttle program.

636. Holmes, Burnham
    EARLY MORNING ROUNDS   Gr. 6-8

    Scholastic/Four Winds, 1982. $9.95.

    > Nick and Jennifer, two third-year medical students, accompany senior physicians and interns on their morning visits with patients.

637. Hoople, Cheryl
    AS I SAW IT: WOMEN WHO LIVED   Gr. 7-10
    THE AMERICAN ADVENTURE

    Dial, 1978. $8.95.

    > Grouped chronologically, these personal accounts taken from the journals, diaries, letters, and speeches of famous and unknown women, give a picture of women's life in American society from the seventeenth century to the present.

638. Isaacman, Clara and Grossman, Joan
    CLARA'S STORY   Gr. 6-8

    Jewish Publication Society of America, 1984. $11.95.

    > An autobiographical account of the Isaacman family's escape from the Nazis in Belgium.

639. Keil, Sally VanWagenen
    THOSE WONDERFUL WOMEN IN   Gr. 8-12
    THEIR FLYING MACHINES

    Rawson, 1979. O.P.

    > Women also flew in World War II, as this lively report makes clear.

640. Kochan, Miriam
    CATHERINE THE GREAT   Gr. 6-9

    St. Martin's, 1977. $6.95.

    > An introductory portrait of the Empress of all the Russias.

641. Koehn, Ilse
MISCHLING, SECOND DEGREE: MY   Gr. 7-8
CHILDHOOD IN NAZI GERMANY

Greenwillow, 1977. $12.88.

> Ilse Koehn became a Hitler Youth Leader, without knowing that she herself was part Jewish.

642. Lawson, Don
THE CHANGING FACE OF THE   Gr. 6-9
CONSTITUTION

Franklin Watts, 1979. $8.40.

> The author examines the shifts in American political and social attitudes that led to a heightened concern for the civil rights of individuals.

643. _____

GERALDINE FERRARO   Gr. 6-9

Messner, 1985. $9.79.

> Lawson traces the life of the first woman vice-presidential nominee from her humble beginnings as the daughter of immigrant parents through her careers as teacher, lawyer and House member to her unsuccessful campaign for the second highest office in the land.

644. Leone, Bruno and O'Neill, M. Teresa, eds.
MALE/FEMALE ROLES: Gr. 9-12
OPPOSING VIEWPOINTS

Greenhaven Press, 1983. $11.95.

> Essays on both sides of the debate over male and female roles. Four to six viewpoints are given on questions such as "How are sex roles established?" and "Do men need liberating?" Betty Friedan and Phyllis Schlafly are among the essayists.

645. Levy, Elizabeth and Miller, Mara
DOCTORS FOR THE PEOPLE   Gr. 6-9

Dell, 1977. $1.25.

> A collection of six interviews with physicians—
> some of them women—who are completely de-
> dicated to their work.

646. Lu Yu
CHINESE WOMEN IN HISTORY AND   Gr. 6-9
LEGEND, V. 1 and V. 2 rev. ed.

A.R.T.S. Inc., 1981. O.P.

> These two slim volumes tell the stories of
> Chinese heroines in history and legend. Al-
> though some of the women led traditional lives,
> they did assert their independence within the
> confines of their society.

647. Madison, Arnold
CARRIE NATION   Gr. 7-9

Thomas Nelson, 1977. O.P.

> This biography—although thin—provides a use-
> ful introduction to the famous campaigner for
> prohibition.

648. Marrin, Albert
THE SEA ROVERS: PIRATES,   Gr. 6-9
PRIVATEERS, AND BUCCANEERS

Atheneum, 1984. $12.95.

> This lively book includes a chapter on women pi-
> rates.

649. Meade, Marion
     FREE WOMAN: THE LIFE AND TIMES   Gr. 7-9
     OF VICTORIA WOODHULL

     Knopf, 1976. $6.95.

              A well-researched, sympathetic account of the
              ninteenth-century feminist who shocked society
              with her independent thought and action.

650. Meyer, Gladys C.
     SOFTBALL FOR GIRLS AND WOMEN   Gr. 9-12

     Scribner, 1982. $12.75.

              A useful manual.

651. Millstein, Beth and Bodin, Jean
     WE, THE AMERICAN WOMEN: Gr. 7-9
     A DOCUMENTARY HISTORY

     Science Research Associates, 1983. $12.67.

              Letters, diary extracts, and other various sources
              provide an examination of women's roles in
              American history.

652. Morrison, Dorothy Nafus
     CHIEF SARAH: SARAH WINNEMUCCA'S   Gr. 7-9
     FIGHT FOR INDIAN RIGHTS

     Atheneum, 1980. $9.95.

              The true story of a Paiute Indian woman who be-
              came an important crusader for her people dur-
              ing the nineteenth century.

653. Myers, Gail Anderson
     A WORLD OF SPORTS FOR GIRLS   Gr. 6-10

     Westminster, 1981. $10.95.

              Anecdotes and facts written to dispel myths and
              promote the image of women athletes.

654. Noble, Iris
CONTEMPORARY WOMEN SCIENTISTS Gr. 7-9
OF AMERICA

Messner, 1979. O.P.

Profiles of nine prominent women scientists, including Margaret Mead and Dixie Lee Ray.

655. O'Connor, Karen
CONTRIBUTIONS OF WOMEN: Gr. 6-9
LITERATURE

Dillon, 1984. $8.95.

Intriguing profiles of five writers; Emily Dickinson, Willa Cather, Pearl S. Buck, May Sarton, and Maya Angelou.

656. O'Kelley, Mattie Lou
FROM THE HILLS OF GEORGIA: All ages
AN AUTOBIOGRAPHY IN PAINTINGS

Atlantic Monthly Press, 1983; dist. by Little, Brown, $14.45.

O'Kelley, who did not start painting until she was 60, includes 28 of her primitive paintings of scenes from her childhood.

657. Peavy, Linda and Smith, Ursula
DREAMS INTO DEEDS: Gr. 6-8
NINE WOMEN WHO DARED

Scribner, 1985. $12.95.

Vignettes from the childhoods of nine famous women, including Rachel Carson, Elizabeth Cady Stanton, Mother Jones and Jane Addams.

658. Ranahan, Demerris
    CONTRIBUTIONS OF WOMEN: MEDICINE   Gr. 6-8

    Dillon, 1981. $8.95.

    > Five women medical pioneers profiled here include Virginia Apgar, founder of the Apgar test for newborn infants' responses and Savitni Ramcharan, who led the research for the birth control pill.

659. Sadler, Catherine Edwards
    SASHA: THE LIFE OF   Gr. 7-10
    ALEXANDRA TOLSTOY

    Putnam, 1982. $9.95.

    > The daughter of Alexander Tolstoy weathered war and the Russian revolution. Frustrated by the aims of Stalinist Russia, she moved to the U.S., where in 1939 she founded the Tolstoy Foundation to aid victims of war and oppression.

660. Schaeder, Catherine
    CONTRIBUTIONS OF WOMEN: MUSIC   Gr. 6-8

    Dillon, 1985. $8.95.

    > Interesting profiles of five women musicians: conductor Antonia Brico, opera singers Beverly Sills and Leontyne Price, composer Ruth Crawford Seeger, and violinist Dylana Jenson.

661. Schneider, Joyce Anne
    FLORA TRISTAN: FEMINIST,   Gr. 9-12
    SOCIALIST, AND FREE SPIRIT

    Morrow, 1980. $11.45.

    > The true story of a nineteenth-century French woman who was born into wealth but was disinherited when her father died because her mother had no marriage certificate. Tristan, radicalized

by poverty and a bad marriage, became a writer and advocate of the rights of women and workers.

662. Scott, John Anthony
WOMAN AGAINST SLAVERY   Gr. 7-9

Harper/Crowell, 1978. $11.95.

A biography of Harriet Beecher Stowe, the author of *Uncle Tom's Cabin*.

663. Seed, Suzanne
FINE TRADES   Gr. 7-12

Follett, 1979. O.P.

An enlightening photo essay on four men and six women who ply a range of highly specialized trades requiring training, skill, and dedication. Among the women are a violin maker, an art conservator, and a professional chef.

664. Selden, Bernice
THE MILL GIRLS: LUCY LARCOM,   Gr. 6-8
HARRIET HANSON, SARAH B. BAGLEY

Atheneum, 1983. $10.95.

A reconstruction of the lives of three nineteenth-century mill workers who became active in the suffrage movement.

665. Shaw, Diana and Berry, Caroline Franklin
OPTIONS: THE FEMALE TEEN'S   Gr. 9-12
GUIDE TO COPING WITH THE PROBLEMS
OF TODAY'S WORLD

Doubleday/Anchor, 1984. $4.95 paper.

Essays on physical and mental health, relationships, education and money, intended to stimulate teenagers to think for themselves.

666. Sherman, Jerry and Hertz, Eric
     WOMAN POWER IN TEXTILE AND   Gr. 7-12
     APPAREL SALES

     Fairchild, 1978. O.P.

           Useful advice about how to get started in the
           fashion business and how to work one's way up.

667. Shiels, Barbara
     WINNERS: WOMEN AND THE   Gr. 6-10
     NOBEL PRIZE

     Dillon, 1985. $14.95.

           Biographies of eight women who have won the
           Nobel prize for literature, science, or peace. In-
           cluded are writers Pearl Buck and Nelly Sachs;
           scientists Barbara McClintock, Dorothy Hodgkin,
           Maria Mayer, and Rosalyn Yaslow; and peace
           prize winners Mother Teresa and Alva Myrdal.

668. Siegel, Alice and McLoone, Marge
     IT'S A GIRL'S GAME TOO   Gr. 5-8

     Holt, Rinehart & Winston, 1980. $9.95.

           This useful guide gives information about
           eighteen different kinds of sports along with help-
           ful comments from famous female athletes.

669. Siegel, Beatrice
     ALICIA ALONZO   Gr. 7-12

     Frederick Warne, 1979. $8.95.

           This is the inspiring story of the Cuban ballerina,
           who was almost permanently blinded by de-
           tached retinas. However, she did fully recover
           and was able to resume her brilliant career. She
           has been a mainstay of the Ballet Nacional de
           Cuba for more than twenty years.

670. _____

AN EYE ON THE WORLD: MARGARET   Gr. 7-9
BOURKE-WHITE, PHOTOGRAPHER

Frederick Warne, 1980. $8.95.

> The life of the remarkable photographer and journalist.

671. _____

LILLIAN WALD OF HENRY STREET   Gr. 7-11

Macmillan, 1983. $12.95.

> Lillian Wald was a turn-of-the-century American pioneer in public health and social reform who founded the Henry Street settlement house in New York City.

672. Smith, Betsy Covington
BREAKTHROUGH: WOMEN IN LAW   Gr. 9-12
Walker, 1984. $12.95.

BREAKTHROUGH: WOMEN IN RELIGION
Walker, 1978. $7.95.

BREAKTHROUGH: WOMEN IN TELEVISION
Walker, 1981. $10.95.

> This series tells young readers about pioneering professional women.

673. Smith, Elizabeth Simpson
BREAKTHROUGH: WOMEN IN AVIATION   Gr. 8-12
Walker, 1981. $10.95.

BREAKTHROUGH: WOMEN IN LAW ENFORCEMENT
Walker, 1982. $11.95.

> *Women in Aviation* profiles nine women including a military air refueling specialist, a cargo pilot, an FAA inspector, and an astronaut. *Women in Law Enforcement* includes ten women in various

jobs such as patrolling the Florida coast or running a prison system.

674. Smith, Tim
JUNIOR WEIGHT TRAINING   Gr. 7-12
AND STRENGTH TRAINING

Athletic Institute, 1985. $11.95; $6.95 paper.

This manual, a primer for beginning weight lifters, offers advice for both boys and girls. It includes exercise plans and tips about proper nutrition.

675. Squires, Bill and Krise, Raymond
IMPROVING WOMEN'S RUNNING   Gr. 10-12

Stephen Greene/Lewis, 1983. $7.95.

A commonsense guide for women who want to become sophisticated about all aspects of running.

676. Stetson, Erlene, ed.
BLACK SISTER: POETRY BY BLACK   Gr. 9-12
AMERICAN WOMEN 1746-1980

Indiana University, 1982. $22.50.

An anthology of poetry written by black American women including Sojourner Truth, Gwendolyn Brooks, and Nikki Giovanni.

677. Swiger, Elinor Porter
WOMEN LAWYERS AT WORK   Gr. 9-12

Messner, 1978. O.P.

A description of the backgrounds and careers of twelve prominent women attorneys.

678. Terry, Walter
FRONTIERS OF DANCE: Gr. 7-10
THE LIFE OF MARTHA GRAHAM

Harper/Crowell, 1975. O.P.

> A detailed and generally flattering biography of
> the idiosyncratic founder of Modern Dance, but
> one which also takes into account some of the
> negative aspects of her personality.

679. Topalian, Elyse
MARGARET SANGER   Gr. 7-10

Frederick Watts, 1984. $9.95.

> A well-organized, well-researched biography of
> the pioneer in the struggle to legalize and pro-
> mote contraception.

680. Western Writers of America
THE WOMEN WHO MADE THE WEST   Gr. 9-12

Doubleday, 1980. $11.95.

> The stories of eighteen women who made the
> trek west in the nineteenth century.

681. Williams, Barbara
BREAKTHROUGH: WOMEN IN ARCHAEOLOGY   Gr. 7-12

Walker, 1980. $9.95.

> Lively profiles of six women who overcame limi-
> tations because of their sex to succeed in a male-
> dominated field.

682. Williams, Selma
DEMETER'S DAUGHTERS   Gr. 7-9

Atheneum, 1976. $9.95.

> A thorough and enlightening look at women in
> America from the seventeenth century to 1776;

American Indian women are included in this survey.

683. Wilson, Ellen
MARGARET FULLER, BLUESTOCKING,   Gr. 6-9
ROMANTIC, REVOLUTIONARY

Farrar, Straus, & Giroux, 1977. $7.95.

A well-written biography of this eighteenth-century intellectual whose ideas and attitudes were most advanced for her time.

684. Zamoyska, Betka
QUEEN ELIZABETH I   Gr. 6-9

McGraw-Hill, 1981. $7.95.

A thoroughly-researched biography which provides insights into Elizabeth's life and her court.

685. Zar, Rose
IN THE MOUTH OF THE WOLF   Gr. 9-12

Jewish Publication Society of America, 1983. $10.95.

The exciting true story of eighteen-year-old Ruska Guterman who, along with her brother, survived the Holocaust. They masqueraded as Polish citizens and Ruska even got a job working in the house of a Colonel in the SS.

AFTERWORD

In 1976 the *Guide to Non-Sexist Children's Books* was the first book published by Academy Chicago Publishers, then called Academy Press Ltd. We published it thinking there was a need for it, since it was compiled from many lists put together by church and nursery school groups; there was no bound volume of lists of non-sexist children's books. We were unprepared for the response to the book, both positive and negative. We were accused by a newspaper columnist of advocating censorship (*Psst, kids,* his column ended, *I know where you can get a hot copy of* Tom Sawyer) and a weekly magazine called upon a child psychologist to condemn the enterprise for reasons which we have mercifully forgotten. To our pleased surprise, this negative publicity in the mass media appeared to encourage positive interest in the book, which also came of course from good reviews in the library periodicals. We sold out our six thousand copies within a few months, and thereby gained a false picture of how oaoy it is for a small press to sell books

Since then we have reprinted the book twice; there are about sixteen thousand copies in print. We now call it the *Guide to Non-Sexist Children's Books Vol. I, to 1976*; the present book covers the years 1976 to 1985. Thus our first book remains in print, as valuable as ever, and we foresee a third volume in 1990.

We are most grateful to our compilers, to Marianne Byrne of our staff, and we wish to issue a belated thanks to all the reviewers, librarians, journalists, teachers, administrators and writers who have given us their whole-hearted support.

The Publishers

SMALL PRESS ADDRESSES

ANNICK PRESS
5519 Yonge St.
Willowdale, Ontario
M2N 5S3

A.R.T.S. INC.
32 Market St.
New York, NY 10002

BLACK MOSS PRESS
P.O. Box 143, Station A
Windsor, Ontario
N9A 6L7

BOOKPEOPLE
2940 Seventh St.
Berkeley, CA 94710

THE CROSSING PRESS
P.O. Box 640
17 W. Main St.
Trumansburg, NY 14886

ED-U PRESS, INC.
P.O. Box 583
Fayetteville, NY 13066

FIREFLY BOOKS
3520 Pharmacy Ave.
Unit 1-C
Scarborough, Ontario
M1W 2T8

LERNER PUBLICATIONS
241 First Ave. North
Minneapolis, MN 55401

LOLLIPOP POWER
P.O. Box 1171
Chapel Hill, NC 27514

MOTHER COURAGE PRESS
1533 Illinois Street
Racine, WI 53405

PARENTING PRESS
7750 31st Ave., N.E.
Seattle, WA 98115

PRESS PORCÉPIC
#235 Market Square
560 Johnson St.
Victoria, British Columbia
V8W 3C6

QUALITY PRESS
3962 South Mariposa
Denver, CO 80110

RAGWEED PRESS
P.O. Box 2023
Charlottetown,
Prince Edward Island
C1A 7N7

THREE TREES PRESS
2 Silver Avenue, 2nd Floor
Toronto, Ontario
M6R 3A2

WESTERN PRAIRIE BOOKS
P.O. Box 2500
Saskatoon, Saskatchewan
S7K 2C4

WINGBOW PRESS
2929 Fifth St.
Berkeley, CA 94710

WOMEN'S PRESS
16 Baldwin St.
Toronto, Ontario
M5T 1L2

ZAMANI PRODUCTIONS
31 W. 31st St.
New York, NY 10001

AUTHOR INDEX

(References are to annotation numbers)

A

Aardema, Verna, 1
Aaron, Chester, 393
Adler, C.S., 168, 169, 394
Adler, David, 2, 327
Adoff, Arnold, 3, 4, 170
Aitkin, Amy, 5
Alcock, Vivian, 171
Alderman, Clifford Lindsey, 602
Alexander, Lloyd, 172, 395
Alexander, Sue, 6
Aliki, 7
Allan, Mabel Esther, 396-398
Allard, Harry, 8
Alter, Judy, 173
Ancona, George, 149
Andersen, Hans Christian, 174
Anderson, Margaret, 175, 399
Andrews, Jan, ed., 176
Angell, Judie, 400, 401
Archambault, John, 91
Arnold, Carolyn, 328
Asch, Frank, 177, 329
Asch, Jan, 329

B

Babbit, Natalie, 178
Bach, Alice, 9
Baehr, Patricia, 402
Bang, Molly, 10, 11
Banish, Roslyn, 12
Barford, Carol, 179
Barger, Gary, 403
Barkhouse, Joyce, 404
Barrington, Elizabeth T., 180
Battles, Edith, 13
Bauer, Carolyn Feller, 14
Baylor, Byrd, 15
Beatty, John, 407
Beatty, Patricia, 181-184, 405-407
Beaudry, Jo, 185
Beckman, Delores, 408
Behrens, June, 150
Bellairs, John, 186
Bemelmans, Ludwig, 16

Berry, Carolyn Franklin, 665
Bertock, Alan, 603
Bess, Clayton, 409, 410
Best, Barbara J., 330
Bethancourt, T. Ernesto, 411
Biddle, Marcia McKenna, 604
Bierhorst, John, 412
Blaine, Marge, 17
Blair, Gwenda, 331
Blegvad, Lenore, 18
Blood, Charles L., 19
Blos, Joan, 413
Blume, Arlene, 605
Bober, Natalie, 606
Bodin, Jean, 651
Bogen, M. Arthur, 414
Bond, Nancy, 415-418
Boyd, Candy Dawson, 419
Boutet de Monvel,
    Louis Maurice, 607
Boutis, Victoria, 187
Bowman, Kathleen, 608
Brady, Esther Wood, 188, 189
Branfield, John, 420
Branscum, Robbie, 421
Brenner, Barbara, 422
Bridgers, Sue Ellen, 423
Briggs, Katherine Mary, 424
Brooks, Jerome, 425
Brooks, Polly Schoyer, 609
Brown, Drollene P., 190
Brown, Fern, 332
Brown, Irene
    Bennett, 191, 426, 427
Brown, Marion Marsh, 428
Buckley, Helen E., 20
Bulla, Clyde Robert, 21, 192
Burch, Robert, 193
Burchard, Peter, 429
Burnett, Frances Hodgson, 194
Burningham, John, 22
Burstein, Chaya M., 195
Byars, Betsy, 196-199

C

Caines, Jeanette Franklin, 23, 24
Calhoun, Mary, 25
Callen, Larry, 200, 201
Calvert, Patricia, 202
Cameron, Eleanor, 430
Campbell, Barbara, 203
Carlson, Dale, 610
Carlson, Nancy, 26
Carrick, Carol, 27, 28
Carris, Joan Davenport, 204
Cavanna, Betty, 431
Cebulash, Mel, 432
Chambers, John, 433
Child Study Association of
    America, 205
Childress, Alice, 434
Christelow, Eileen, 29
Clapp, Patricia, 333
Clark, Ann Nolan, 206
Cleary, Beverly, 207
Cleaver, Bill, 436-438
Cleaver, Vera, 435-438
Clements, Bruce, 439
Clifford, Eth, 208, 440
Clifton, Lucille, 30, 31
Clymer, Eleanor, 209, 210
Coerr, Eleanor, 32, 334, 335
Cohen, Barbara, 211, 212,
    441, 442
Cohen, Caron Lee, 33
Cohen, Miriam, 34
Cole, Joanna, 151
Collard, Alexandra, 611
Collier, Christopher, 443, 444
Collier, James Lincoln, 443, 444
Collura, Mary Ellen Lang, 445
Colman, Hila, 446
Conford, Ellen, 213, 447, 448
Conrad, Pamela, 449
Cooney, Caroline B., 450
Cooper, Ilene, 612
Cooper, Susan, 451
Corbett, Scott, 214
Corcoran, Barbara, 215, 452
Craft, Ruth, 35
Cresswell, Helen, 453

Cross, Gillian, 454
Cunningham, Julia, 455
Currimbhoy, Nayana, 613

D

Daugherty, Lynn B., 614
Davidson, Margaret, 336
Davis, Andrew, 216
Davis, Diane, 36
Davis, Gibbs, 456
Delton, Judy, 37, 38
dePaola, Tomie, 40, 41
DePauw, Linda Grant, 615, 616
Dickerson, Louise, 42
Djabbaroff, Ruby, 635
Dixon, Paige, 457
Dodd, Wayne, 458
Doty, Jean Slaughter, 217, 218
Douglass, Barbara, 43
Duncombe, Frances Riker, 459
Dunlop, Eileen, 219
Dunnahoo, Terry, 617
Dygard, Thomas, 460

E

Eagen, Andrea Boroff, 618
Edelman, Elaine, 44
Eige, Lillian E., 461
Ellis, Ella Tharp, 462
Ellis, Melvin Richard, 463
Elmore, Patricia, 220
Emberlin, Diane, 337
English, Betty Lou, 338, 619
Epstein, Anne Merrick, 464
Epstein, Vivian Sheldon, 152
Etherington, Frank, 221
Evernden, Margery, 465
Evslin, Bernard, 466

F

Faber, Doris, 620
Facklam, Margery, 621
Fairfield, Lesley, 153
Fanshawe, Elizabeth, 45
Farber, Norma, 46
Faulkner, Margaret, 339
Feldman, Alan, 222

Fitzhugh, Louise, 467
Flory, Jane, 223, 224
Flynn, Charlotte, 468
Flooner, Michael, 340
Forbes, Tom H., 469
Forman, James, 470
Fowler, Carol, 341
Fox, Mary Virginia, 342, 343, 622
Francis, Dorothy Brenner, 471
Frayne, Trent, 623
Freedman, Russell, 344, 624
Fritz, Jean, 625
Fusco, Marina, 626
Fusco, Patricia, 626

G
Gaeddert, Lou Ann Bigge, 627
Gage, Wilson, 47
Galbraith, Kathryn Osebold, 472
Galdone, Paul, 48
Gallaz, Christophe, 249
Garcia, Ann O'Neal, 473
Garrigue, Sheila, 225, 474
Gates, Doris, 226
Gauch, Patricia Lee, 227
Giff, Patricia Reilly, 228, 229
Gilchrist, Theo E., 49
Gilham, Bill, 230
Girard, Linda Walvoord, 154, 155
Girion, Barbara, 475
Gleasner, Diana C., 628
Goldberger, Judith, 231
Golden, Flora, 345
Goldman, Susan, 50
Goldreich, Esther, 346-350
Goldreich, Gloria, 346-350
Goodall, John, 51
Gordon, Ruth, 156
Gordon, Shirley, 52
Gordon, Sol, 156
Gornick, Vivian, 629
Grant, Anne, 53
Greaves, Margaret, 232
Greene, Bette, 476
Greene, Carol, 351
Greene, Constance, 233, 234

Greenfield, Eloise, 54, 55, 352, 353, 630
Greenwald, Sheila, 235
Griffin, Judith Berry, 236
Grimm, Jacob, 56
Grimm, Wilhelm, 56
Gross, Ruth, 57
Grossman, Joan, 638
Guernsey, JoAnn Bren, 477
Gutman, Bill, 354

H
Haber, Louis, 631
Hall, Lynn, 478-481
Hall, Malcolm, 58
Hamerstrom, Frances, 237
Hamilton, Virginia, 482-485
Haney, Lynn, 355, 632
Hanson, June Andrea, 486
Harris, Christie, 238, 239
Harris, Robie, 240
Hartling, Peter, 241
Haskins, James, 633, 634
Hautzig, Deborah, 487
Hautzig, Esther, 356
Hearne, Betsy Gould, 242
Hendrickson, Karen, 59
Hertz, Eric, 666
Herzig, Alison, 357
Hewitt, Marsha, 488
Hickman, Janet, 489
Hickman, Martha Whitmore, 60
Highwater, Jamake, 490
Hilgartner, Beth, 491
Hinton, S.E., 492
Hoban, Lillian, 61
Hodgman, Ann, 635
Hoff, Sydney, 62
Holland, Isabelle, 493
Hollander, Phyllis, 358
Holmes, Burnham, 636
Homan, Dianne, 157
Hooks, William, 243
Hoople, Cheryl, compiler, 637
Hoover, H.M., 494
Howard, Jane R., 63
Hughes, Monica, 495

Hughes, Shirley, 64-66
Hunt, Irene, 496
Hunter, Mollie, 497
Hurmence, Belinda, 498, 499
Hurwitz, Johanna, 244-246
Hutchins, H.J., 247, 248
Hyman, Trina Schart, 359

I
Ichikawa, Satomi, 67
Innocenti, Roberto, 249
Irwin, Hadley, 250, 251, 500
Isaacman, Clara, 638
Isadora, Rachel, 68, 69

J
Jacobs, William Jay, 252, 360
Jacques, Faith, 70
Jeffers, Susan, 71
Jewell, Nancy, 72
Johnson, Dorothy M., 501
Johnston, Norma, 502, 503
Jonas, Ann, 73
Jones, Betty Milsaps, 361
Jukes, Mavis, 74

K
Karl, Jean, 253
Kay, Mara, 254
Kaye, Geraldine, 255
Keil, Sally VanWagenen, 639
Kennedy, Stephanie, 504
Kennemore, Tim, 505
Kerr, M.E., 506
Kesselman, Wendy, 75
Ketchum, Lynne, 185
King-Smith, Dick, 256
Klein, Norma, 76, 257, 507
Kleitch, Christel, 258, 259
Knotts, Howard, 77
Knox-Wagner, Elaine, 41
Knudson, R.R., 508, 509
Kochan, Miriam, 640
Koehn, Ilse, 641
Krise, Raymond, 675
Krementz, Jill, 362, 363
Kroll, Steven, 78

Krumens, Anita, 260
Kurelek, William, 261

L
L'Engle, Madeline, 511
Lampman, Evelyn Sibly, 262
Lane, Carolyn, 263
Langner, Nola, 79
Langton, Jane, 264
Lasky, Kathryn, 80, 158,
    265, 510
Lawson, Don, 642, 643
Layman, Constance, 266
Leder, Jane Mersky, 364
Lee, John, 159, 160
Lee, Susan, 159, 160
Leiner, Katherine, 161
Leone, Bruno, 644
Levinson, Riki, 81
Levitin, Sonia, 82
Levy, Elizabeth, 83,
    267, 646
Lindgren, Astrid, 268
Lindsey, Treska, 84
Lingard, Joan, 512
Link, Martin A., 19
Little, Lessie Jones, 630
Lively, Penelope, 513
Long, Earlene, 162
Lord, Athena, 514
Love, Sandra, 269
Lovejoy, Bahija, 442
Lowry, Lois, 270, 271, 515
Lu Yu, 646
Lundgren, Hal, 365
Lurie, Alison, 272

M
MacGregor, Ellen, 273
MacLachlan, Patricia, 274, 275
MacLeod, Charlotte, 516
McClenathan, Louise, 85
McCully, Emily Arnold, 86
McGovern, Ann, 87, 366, 367
McKinley, Robin, 517, 518
McLaughlin, Patricia, 88
McLoone, Marge, 668

McPhail, David, 89, 90
Mackay, Claire, 488
Madison, Arnold, 647
Madison, Winifred, 519, 520
Magnuson, James, 521
Mahey, Margaret, 522
Mali, Jane, 357
Mark, Jan, 523
Marrin, Albert, 648
Martin, Bill, 91
Marzollo, Jean, 92
Mathis, Sharon Bell, 276, 524
Mauser, Pat Rhoads, 277
Mayer, Mercer, 93
Mazer, Harry, 525-527
Mazer, Norma Fox, 278, 528
Meade, Marion, 649
Meltzer, Milton, 368, 369
Merrill, Susan, 94
Meyer, Carolyn, 529, 530
Meyer, Gladys C., 650
Meyers, Bernice, 279
Meyers, Susan, 280
Miles, Betty, 281, 282, 531
Miller, Mara, 645
Miller, Margaret, 370
Miller, Sandy, 532
Mills, Claudia, 533
Millstein, Beth, 651
Minard, Rosemary, 283
Moeri, Louise, 534
Monjo, F.N., 353
Moore, Sheila, 95
Morrison, Dorothy Nafus, 371, 652
Moskin, Marietta, 284
Munsch, Robert, 96
Murphy, Joan Brisson, 97
Murphy, Shirley Rousseau, 98, 285
Myers, Gail Anderson, 653
Myers, Walter Dean, 536

N
Naylor, Phyllis Reynolds, 286
Ness, Evaline, 99
Newman, Robert, 287
Newton, Suzanne, 537, 538
Nichol, bp, 100

Nixon, Joan Lowery, 288
Noble, Iris, 654
Nolan, Madeena Spray, 101

O
O'Brien, Robert C., 539
O'Connor, Jane, 289
O'Connor, Karen, 372, 655
O'Dell, Scott, 290, 540
O'Kelley, Mattie Lou, 656
O'Neal, Zibby, 541
O'Neill, M. Teresa, 644
Okimoto, Jean Davies, 291
Olney, Ross, 373
Oppenheim, Joanne, 102
Ormerod, Jan, 103, 104
Ormondroyd, Edward, 105
Oxenbury, Helen, 292

P
Pantell, Dora F., 273
Park, Ruth, 542
Parry, Marian, 106
Pascal, Francine, 293
Paterson, Katherine, 294, 295, 543, 544
Patterson, Lillie, 374
Peavy, Linda, 657
Peck, Richard, 545-547
Peterson, Joanne Whitehouse, 163
Peterson, P.J., 548
Petrie, Dorothea G., 521
Pevsner, Stella, 549
Peyton, K.M., 550
Pfeffer, Susan Beth, 551
Phillips, Betty Lou, 375
Phipson, Joan, 552
Piekarski, Vicki, 553
Pierce, Tamora, 296
Pogrebin, Letty Cotten, 297
Pomerantz, Charlotte, 107
Porte, Barbara Ann, 108
Price, Susan, 554

Q
Quackenbush, Robert, 109
Quinn-Harkin, Janet, 555

R

Rabe, Bernice, 110, 298, 299
Ranahan, Demerris, 658
Raskin, Ellen, 556
Ray, Deborah Kogan, 111
Ray, Mary, 557
Rench, Janice E., 380
Rice, Eve, 112
Riordan, James, 558
Roberts, Maurice, 164
Roche, Patricia K., 300
Rockwell, Harlow, 113
Rockwood, Joyce, 559
Rodgers, Raboo, 560
Rodowsky, Colby, 561
Rogers, Fred, 165
Ruchman, Ivy, 301
Rylant, Cynthia, 114, 115

S

Sadler, Catherine Edwards, 659
St. George, Judith, 130, 302, 562
Sallis, Susan, 563
Saunders, Susan, 376
Schaeder, Catherine, 660
Schertle, Alice, 116
Schick, Eleanor, 117
Schlee, Ann, 564
Schneider, Joyce Anne, 661
Scott, Carol J., 565
Scott, John Anthony, 662
Sebestyen, Ouida, 566, 567
Seed, Suzanne, 663
Selden, Bernice, 664
Selfridge, Oliver G., 303
Sendak, Maurice, 118
Sharmat, Marjorie Weinman, 119-121
Shaw, Diana, 665
Shecter, Ben, 122
Sherman, Jerry, 666
Shiels, Barbara, 667
Shreve, Susan Richards, 304, 305
Siegel, Alice, 668
Siegel, Beatrice, 669-671
Silverman, Maida, 123
Simon, Marcia L., 306

Simon, Norma, 124, 166, 307
Singer, Isaac Beshevis, 568
Singer, Marilyn, 308, 569
Skorpen, Liesel Moak, 125
Slepian, Jan, 570, 571
Smith, Betsy Covington, 672
Smith, Doris Buchanan, 309
Smith, Elizabeth Simpson, 673
Smith, Lucia, 126
Smith, Samantha, 377
Smith, Tim, 674
Smith, Ursula, 657
Snow, Pegeen, 127
Snyder, Carol, 128
Sobol, Rose, 378
Spurr, Elizabeth, 129
Squires, Bill, 675
Stanek, Lou Willet, 572
Stanley, Diane, 131
Stearns, Pamela, 310
Stecher, Miriam B., 132
Stephens, Paul, 258, 259
Steptoe, John, 133
Stetson, Erlene, 676
Stevens, Carla, 134
Stewart, A.C., 311
Stone, Bruce, 573
Stone, Josephine Rector, 574
Stoutenburg, Adrien, 312
Strauss, Victoria, 575
Streiber, Whitley, 576
Sullivan, George, 379
Sutton, Larry, 577
Swede, George, 313
Swiger, Elinor Porter, 677
Szabo, Joseph, 578

T

Taylor, Janet Lisle, 579
Taylor, Mildred, 580
Terkel, Susan N. 380
Terris, Susan, 314
Terry, Walter, 678
Thatcher, Alida M., 381
Thiele, Colin, 315
Thomas, Jane Resh, 135
Thomas, Joyce Carol, 581, 582

Thomas, Marlo, 316
Thompson, Jean, 317
Thrasher, Crystal, 583
Tinkleman, Murray, 167, 382
Tolan, Stephanie S., 584, 585
Tolle, Jean Bashor, 318
Topalian, Elyse, 679
Towne, Mary, 586
Tudor, Bethany, 383
Turkle, Brinton, 136
Turnbull, Ann, 587
Tusa, Tricia, 137

U
Uchida, Yoshiko, 588

V
Van Woerkom, Dorothy,
    138-139, 319
Vincent, Gabrielle, 140
Viorst, Judith, 141
Vogel, Ilse-Margaret, 142
Voigt, Cynthia, 589, 590

W
Wachter, Oralee, 384
Wain, John, 591
Waldron, Ann, 320, 321
Walker, Lou Ann, 385
Wallace, Barbara Brooks, 322
Walsh, Jill Paton, 592
Walter, Mildred Pitts, 143, 593
Weiner, Sandra, 386
Wells, Rosemary, 144
Western Writers of America, 680
Westfall, Robert, 594
White, Ellen, 595
Whitmore, Arvella, 323
Wilder, Cherry, 596
Wilkinson, Brenda Scott, 597
Williams, Barbara, 681
Williams, Jay, 324
Williams, Selma, 682
Williams, Vera B., 145, 146
Wilson, Dorothy Clark, 387
Wilson, Ellen, 683
Winthrop, Elizabeth, 325

Wolde, Gunilla, 147
Wolf, Bernard, 388, 389
Woods, Geraldine, 390
Woods, Harold, 390

Y
Yarbro, Chelsea Quinn, 598
Yeoman, John, 148
Yep, Laurence, 599, 600
Yolen, Jane, 326

Z
Zamoyska, Betka, 684
Zar, Rose, 685
Zeck, Gerry, 391
Zemach, Margo, 392
Zindel, Bonnie, 601
Zindel, Paul, 601

TITLE INDEX

(References are to annotation numbers)

A

Abigail Adams, 159
Absolute Zero, 453
Accident, The, 27
After Pa Was Shot, 173
Al (exandra) the Great, 233
Alanna: The First Adventure, 296
Alexandra the Rock Eater, 138
Alfred Summer, The, 570
Alicia Alonzo, 669
All It Takes is Practice, 281
All Kinds of Families, 166
All This Wild Land, 206
All Those Mothers at the
    Manger, 46
All Together Now, 423
All-in-All: A Biography of
    George Eliot, 627
Almost Grown, 578
Amelia Mixed the Mustard, 99
Amy Goes Fishing, 92
Amy: The Story of a Deaf
    Child, 385
Anastasia Again, 270
Anastasia, Ask Your Analyst, 270
Anastasia At Your Service, 270
Anastasia Krupnik, 270
Anastasia Morningstar and
    Crystal Butterfly, 247
Animal Fathers, 344
Anna and the Seven Swans, 123
Anna Banana and Me, 18
Anna, Grandpa, and the Big
    Storm, 134
Anna's Silent World, 388
Annapurna: A Woman's
    Place, 605
Annie Oakley & the World
    of Her Time, 602
Answer Me, Answer Me, 426
Anywhere Else But Here, 439
Are You In the House Alone?, 545
Arilla Sundown, 482
Arthur's Honey Bear, 61
As I Saw It: Women Who Lived the
    American Adventure, 637
Ask Me No Questions, 564
Ask Me What My Mother
    Does, 161
Autumn Street, 271

B

Baby and I Can Play, 59
Baby for Max, A, 158
Bad Dreams of a Good Girl, 304
Bagthorpes Abroad, The, 453
Bagthorpes Unlimited, 453
Bagthorpes vs. the World, 453
Balancing Girl, The, 110
Barbara Jordan: The Great
    Lady from Texas, 164
Barely Undercover, 414
Bargain Bride, 262
Beat the Turtle Drum, 234
Beauty, 517
Becky and the Bear, 139
Before the Lark, 427
Before the Supreme Court:
    The Story of Belva Ann
    Lockwood, 617
Beggar Queen, The, 395
Bella Abzug, 620
Beloved Benjamin is
    Waiting, 253
Benny, 211
Benny Bakes a Cake, 112
Ben's Trumpet, 68
Best Bad Thing, The, 588
Best Mom in the World, The, 41
Best of Enemies, The, 415
Betsy and the Chicken Pox, 147
Betsy's First Day at Nursery
    School, 147
Better Safe than Sorry
    Book, A, 156
Betty Friedan: A Voice
    for Women's Rights, 368
Between Dark and Daylight, 583
Between Friends, 225
Beyond the Divide, 510

Big Balloon Race, 32
Big Dipper Marathon, The, 425
Big Man and the Burnout, 409
Big Sister Tells Me That I'm
   Black, 3
Billy Bedamned, Long Gone
   By, 181
Bimwili & the Zimwi: A Tale
   from Zanzibar, 1
Bitter Herbs and Honey, 441
Black Sister: Poetry by Black
   American Women 1746-
   1980, 676
Boy Who Wanted a Family, The, 52
Boys Have Feelings Too: Growing
   Up Male for Boys, 610
Bravo, Ernest and Celestine, 140
Breadsticks and Blessing
   Places, 419
Breakfast Time, Ernest and
   Celestine, 140
Breaking Tradition: The Story
   of Louise Nevelson, 606
Breakthrough: Women in
   Archaeology, 681
Breakthrough: Women in
   Aviation, 673
Breakthrough: Women in Law, 672
Breakthrough: Women in
   Law Enforcement, 673
Breakthrough: Women in
   Religion, 672
Breakthrough: Women in
   Science, 628
Breakthrough: Women in
   Television, 672
Breakthrough: Women in
   Writing, 628
Bridge to Terabithia, 294
Buffalo Woman, 501
Bundle of Sticks, A, 277
Bus Ride, 72
Busybody Nora, 244
But What About Me?, 269
By Crumbs, It's Mine, 182

C

Cable Car to Catastrophe, 109
Call Me Danica, 519
Captain Morgana Mason, 471
Carla Goes to Court, 185
Carlota, 540
Carrie Hepple's Garden, 35
Carrie Nation, 647
Case of the Baker Street
   Irregulars, The, 287
Casey and the Great Idea, 288
Catherine the Great, 640
Chair for My Mother, A, 145
Changeover, The, 522
Changing Face of the
   Constitution, The, 642
Changing Times, 505
Chase the Sun, 532
Cheerleader, The, 507
Chief Sarah: Sarah
   Winnemucca's Fight for
   Indian Rights, 652
Child of the Owl, 599
Children of the Sun, 581
Children of the Wild
   West, 624
Childtimes: A Three
   Generational Memoir, 630
Chinese Women in History
   and Legend, 646
Chinwe, 429
Chris Evert, The Young
   Champion, 632
Clara's Story, 638
Clearance, The, 512
Clever Gretchen, and Other
   Forgotten Folk Tales, 272
Colonel and Me, The, 433
Come Away from the Water,
   Shirley, 22
Come Sing, Jimmy Jo, 543
Come Spring, 472
Comfort Herself, 255
Connie's New Eyes, 389
Conrad's War, 216
Contemporary Women
   Scientists of America, 654

Contributions of Women:
  Literature, 655
Contributions of Women:
  Medicine, 658
Contributions of Women:
  Music, 660
Contributions of Women:
  Science, 337
Coretta Scott King, 374
Country of Broken Stone, 416
Country Tale, A, 131
Courage to Adventure: Stories
  of Boys and Girls Growing Up
  With America, 205
Cowgirl, 167
Cracker Jackson, 196
Crumb, The, 217
Cute Is a Four Letter Word, 549

D

Daddy, 23
Daddy and Ben Together, 132
Daddy Is A Monster…
  Sometimes, 133
Dad's Back, 103
Daisy Hooee Nampeyo, 341
Danbury's Burning! The Story of
  Sybil Ludington's Ride, 53
Dancing Feathers, 258
Dancing Sun, 176
Dangerous Beat, 468
Danza!, 478
Dark Didn't Catch Me, The, 583
Dark is Rising, The, 451
Darlene, 54
Day of the Blizzard, 284
Delikon, The, 494
Demeter's Daughters, 682
Dicey's Song, 589
Dinky Hocker Shoots Smack, 506
Doctors for the People, 645
Dodo Every Day, 142
Dolly Parton: Country
  Goin' to Town, 376
Don't Forget Michael, 317
Doris Fein: Superspy, 411
Dorothea Lange: Life Through
  the Camera, 369
Double Life of Pocahontas,
  The, 625
Doug Meets the Nutcracker, 243
Drawn from New England: Tasha
  Tudor. A Portrait in Words
  and Pictures, 383
Dreadful Future of Blossom
  Culp, The, 546
Dream Keeper, The, 465
Dreams into Deeds, 657
Duchess, 393
Dudley and the Birdman, 313
Dusty, 79

E

Early Morning Rounds, 636
Eat Your Peas, Louise!, 127
Edgemont, 119
Eleanor Roosevelt: A Life
  of Happiness and Tears, 360
Eliza Pinckney, 160
Elizabeth Catches a Fish, 135
Emma, 75
Emma's Pet, 89
End of a Dark Road, 583
End to Perfect, An, 537
Equal Justice: A Biography of
  Sandra Day O'Connor, 390
Ernest and Celestine, 140
Ernest and Celestine's Picnic, 140
Eternal Spring of Mr. Ito, The, 474
Euphonia and the Flood, 25
Everett Anderson's Friend, 30
Express Train to Trouble, 109
Eye on the World:
  Margaret Bourke-White,
  Photographer, 670

F

Faithfully, Tru, 402
Famous Women Tennis
  Players, 623
Faraway Island, The, 215
Farm Morning, 90
Feeling Mad Feeling Sad
  Feeling Bad Feeling Glad, 87

Feeling Safe Feeling Strong:
How to Avoid Sexual Abuse
and What to Do If It Happens
to You, 380
Feelings, 97
Figure in the Shadows, The, 186
Fine Soft Day, A, 470
Fine Trades, 663
First Serve, 586
First Snow, 86
First the Egg, 534
Fishman and Charly, 456
Flora Tristan: Feminist,
Socialist, and Free Spirit, 661
Flowers of Anger, 479
Flunking of Joshua T.
Bates, The, 305
Fly into Danger, 552
Fog Drift Morning, 111
Forecast, 58
Founding Mothers: Women of
America in the Revolutionary
Era, 615
Foundling, The, 27
Four Horses for Tishtray, 598
Fox Farm, 219
Fox in Winter, The, 420
Fragile Flag, 264
Free to Be You and Me, 316
Free Woman: The Life and Times
of Victoria Woodhull, 649
French Detection, The, 320
Friends, 67
From the Hills of Georgia: An
Autobiography in Paintings, 656
From Where I Stand, 554
Frontiers of Dance: The Life of
Martha Graham, 678
Fun With Toddlers, 59

G
Gabriel's Girl, 502
Gathering of Days, 413
The General, 221
Genessee Queen, The, 520
George the Babysitter, 64
Geraldine Ferraro, 643

Get Away Car, The, 209
Getting On With It, 571
Ghost Belonged to Me, The, 546
Ghost-Eye Tree, The, 91
Ghost Island, 263
Ghosts I Have Been, 546
Gift of the Pirate Queen, The, 228
Girl Called Al, A, 233
Girl Called Bob and a Horse
Called Yoki, A, 203
Girl Called Boy, A, 498
Girl Groups, 603
Girl Who Had No Name, The, 298
Girl Who Wouldn't Get
Married, The, 57
Girl With Spunk, The, 302
Glory in the Flower, 503
Goat in the Rug, The, 19
Going to Daycare, 165
Golda Meir Story, The, 336
Golden Venture, The, 223
Good as New, 43
Good-bye, Arnold, 300
Good-bye, Chicken Little, 197
Good Stones, 464
Good Wife, Good Wife, 42
Gorilla Signs Love, The, 422
Grandma Is Somebody
Special, 50
Grandmamma's Joy, 55
Great Gilly Hopkins, The, 295
Great-Grandfather, the Baby
and Me, 77
Great Pete Penney, The, 318
Great Pistachio Case, The, 266
Great Skinner Strike, The, 584
Green is for Galanx, 574
Greenwitch, 451
Grey King, The, 451
Grey Lady and the Strawberry
Snatcher, The, 10
Guess Who My Favorite Person
Is, 15

H
Hadder MacColl, 202
Half-Birthday Party, The, 107

Half Nelson, Full Nelson, 573
Halfway Up the Mountain, 49
Halloween Pumpkin Smasher,
    The, 130
Hammerhead Light, The, 315
Handles, 523
Hand-Me-Down Kid, The, 293
Happiest Ending, The, 588
Harry's Mom, 108
Hazel Rye, 436
Hazel's Amazing Mother, 144
Helping Out, 149
Heraclea: A Legend of Warrior
    Women, 466
Hero and the Crown, The, 518
Hester the Jester, 122
Hey, Didi Darling, 504
Hey, Dollface, 487
History of Women for
    Children, 152
Hockey Girls, 214
Home, 242
Home Alone, 117
Home Before Long, 230
Homecoming, 589
Homeward the Arrow's Flight, 428
The Horsemaster, 569
Hot off the Press!, 370
House in Norham Gardens,
    The, 513
House With a Clock in Its Walls,
    The, 186
Hugo and the Princess Nena, 462
Hundred Penny Box, The, 276
Hungry Woman, The, 412

I
I Am A Big Help, 106
I Am the Running Girl, 170
I Can Be a Truck Driver, 150
I Have A Sister—My Sister Is
    Deaf, 163
I Know You, Al, 233
I Love My Baby Sister (Most of
    the Time), 44
I Love Softball, 330

I Love to Dance: A True Story
    About Tony Jones, 391
I Skate, 339
I Want to Be a Fisherman, 386
I Want to Tell You About My
    Baby, 12
I Will Be a Doctor: The Story
    of America's First Woman
    Physician, 387
Ike and Mama and the Once-A-
    Year Suit, 128
I'm Busy Too, 124
I'm Deborah Sampson: A
    Soldier in the War of the
    Revolution, 333
I'm Not Your Other Half, 450
Improving Women's
    Running, 675
In Christina's Toolbox, 157
In the Face of Danger, 254
In Summer Light, 541
In the Mouth of the Wolf, 685
In the Shadow of the Bear, 562
Indira Gandhi, 613
Into the Painted Bear Lair, 310
IOU's, 566
Isis Pedlar, 495
Island Keeper, The, 525
It Can't Hurt Forever, 308
It's a Girl's Game Too, 668

J
Jackaroo, 590
Jacob Have I Loved, 544
Jane Goodall, 334
Janet Guthrie, First Woman
    at Indy, 373
Janet Guthrie, Foot to
    the Floor, 342
Jar of Dreams, A, 588
Jerome the Babysitter, 29
Jim Meets the Thing, 34
Joan of Arc, 607
Johnny Castleseed, 105
Johnny's Egg, 162
Journey of the Shadow
    Bairns, 175

Journey to Almost There, 477
Journey to the Soviet Union, 377
Julia and the Hand of God, 430
Julia's Magic, 430
Julie's Daughter, 561
Julie's Summer, 583
Junior Weight Training and
   Strength Training, 674
Just One Friend, 480
Justice Sandra Day O'Connor, 343
Just Some Weeds in the
   Wilderness, 183
Just Us Women, 24

K
Kate Crackernuts, 424
Katherine Dunham, 633
Katy Did It, 187
Keeping Days, The, 503
Kentucky Daughter, 565
Kestrel, The, 395
Kidnapping of Mister Huey,
   The, 461

L
Labor: Contributions of
   Women, 604
Ladies Were Not Expected, 371
Laura Ingalls Wilder, 331
Law of Gravity, The, 245
Left-Handed Shortstop, 229
Legend Days, 490
Legend of Bluebonnet, The, 39
Lena Horne, 634
Let Me Hear the Music, 179
Let the Circle Be Unbroken, 580
Let's Go/Allons-Y!, 153
Letter, the Witch, and the Ring, 186
Liberation of Clementine
   Tipton, The, 224
Liberation of Tansy Warner,
   The, 585
Life With Working Parents, 356
Light in the Mountain, 399
Like Jake and Me, 74
Lilith Summer, The, 250
Lillian Wald of Henry Street, 671

Listen for the Fig Tree, 524
Little Britches Rodeo, 382
Little Love, A, 483
Littlest Leaguer, 62
Liza Lou and the Yeller Belly
   Swamp, 93
Lizzie's Floating Shop, 591
Long Meg, 283
Looking Glass Factor, The, 231
Louanne Pig in Making the
   Team, 26
Louanne Pig in the Mysterious
   Valentine, 26
Louanne Pig in the Perfect
   Family, 26
Louanne Pig in the
   Talent Show, 26
Love Match, 555
Luck of Texas McCoy, The, 529
Luckie Star, The, 321
Lucy Mastermind, 222
Ludell, 597
Ludell and Willie, 597
Ludell's New York Time, 597

M
M.C. Higgins, the Great, 484
M.V. Sexton Speaking, 538
Machine Gunners, The, 594
Madeline's Christmas, 16
Magic of the Glits, The, 168
Magic Porridge Pot, The, 48
Magnum Fault, 560
Male/Female Roles: Opposing
   Viewpoints, 644
Mandy's Grandmother, 125
Marathon Miranda, 325
Margaret Fuller: Bluestocking,
   Romantic, Revolutionary, 683
Margaret Sanger, 679
Mariah Delaney Lending
   Library, The, 235
Marina and Ruby, 626
Marked By Fire, 582
Maroo of the Winter Caves, 587
Martina Navratilova, 364

Mary Lou Retton: A
  Biography, 379
Mary Lou Retton: Gold
  Metal Gymnast, 365
Mary McLeod Bethune, 352
Master Rosalind, 407
Matter of Principle, A, 551
Maudie and Me and the Dirty
  Book, 282
Maurice Sendak's Really
  Rosie: Starring the
  Nutshell Kids, 118
Max, 69
"Me and You and a Dog Named
  Blue", 452
Megan's Beat, 572
Mermaid's Three Wisdoms,
  The, 326
Merry Christmas, Ernest and
  Celestine, 140
Messy Baby, 103
Mill Girls, The, 664
Millicent the Magnificent, 9
Mills Down Below, The, 396
Miranda, 137
Mischling, Second Degree: My
  Childhood in Nazi Germany, 641
Miss Maggie, 114
Miss Nelson Has a Field Day, 8
Miss Nelson Is Back, 8
Miss Nelson Is Missing, 8
Miss Pickerell Takes the Bull
  by the Horns, 273
Morgan for Melinda, A, 226
Mother, Aunt Susan, and Me: The
  First Fight for Women's
  Rights, 252
Mother Teresa, 351
Mouse Woman and the Vanished
  Princess, 238
Mrs. Claus's Crazy Christmas, 78
Mrs. Fish, Ape, and Me, the Dump
  Queen, 278
Mrs. Gaddy and the Fast-Growing
  Vine, 47
Mrs. Gaddy and the Ghost, 47
Mrs. Minetta's Car Pool, 129

Mrs. Peloki's Snake, 102
Much Ado About Aldo, 246
Music Lessons for Alex, 328
Mustard Seed of Magic, 503
My Body Is Private, 154
My Daddy Don't Go To Work, 101
My Friend William Moved Away, 60
My Island Grandma, 80
My Mom Got a Job, 126
My Mom Travels a Lot, 14
My Mama Needs Me, 143
My Mother Is Not Married to My
  Father, 291
My Mother is the Smartest Woman
  in the World, 210
My Mother Sends Her Wisdom, 85
My Nursery School, 113
My Own Private Sky, 408
My Two Feet, 116

N

Nadia the Willful, 6
Naughty Nancy Goes to
  School, 51
Necklace of Fallen Stars, A, 491
Net to Catch the Wind, A, 232
New Baby, The, 165
New Baby at Your House, The, 151
New Neighbors for Nora, 244
New Women in Art and
  Dance, 608
New Women in
  Entertainment, 608
New Women in Media, 608
New Women in Medicine, 608
New Women in Politics, 608
New Women in Social
  Sciences, 608
Night Cry, 286
Night Dive, 366
Night Journey, The, 265
Night Swimmers, The, 198
No More Secrets for Me, 384
Nobody Else Can Walk It For
  You, 548
Nobody's Family is Going to
  Change, 467

Nora and Mrs. Mind-Your-Own-
    Business, 244
Northern Nativity, A: Christmas
    Dreams of a Prairie Boy, 261
Now One Foot, Now the Other, 40

O

Of Love, Death, and Other
    Journeys, 493
Oh Boy! Babies!, 357
Oliver Button is a Sissy, 41
Oma, 241
On the Edge, 454
Once in a While Hero, The, 169
100 Greatest Women in Sports, 358
101 Things to Do With a Baby, 104
One Proud Summer, 488
Only Love, 563
Options: The Female Teen's
    Guide to Coping with the
    Problems of Today's World, 665
Ordinary Jack, 453
Orphan Train, 521
Orphans, The, 299
Our Golda: The Story of Golda
    Meir, 327
Over Sea, Under Stone, 451

P

P.J. Clover, Private Eye, 280
Paper Bag Princess, The, 96
Parcel of Patterns, A, 592
Part-Time Boy, 180
Pearl in the Egg, 319
Pearl's Promise, 177
Peppermints in the Parlor, 322
Perfect Balance: The Story of
    an Elite Gymnast, 355
Phoebe and the General, 236
Picture Story of Nancy Lopez, 375
Pilgrimage, The, 512
Pinballs, The, 199
Place to Come Back To, A, 417
Playing Beatie Bow, 542
Porcelain Pagoda, The, 535
Practical Princess, The, 324
Prairie Songs, 449

President's Daughter, The, 595
Princess of the Chameln, 596

Q

Queen and Rosie Randall,
    The, 292
Queen Eleanor: Independent
    Spirit of the Medieval World, 609
Queen Elizabeth I, 684
Queen of Hearts, 437
Queen's Nose, The, 256
Quincy's Harvest, 469

R

Rabbit for Easter, A, 28
Rachel, 45
Rachel and Obadiah, 136
Rachel's Legacy, 446
Racing Against the Odds, 332
Raising a Racket: Rosie
    Casals, 381
Ramona and Her Father, 207
Ramona and Her Mother, 207
Ramona Forever, 207
Ramona Quimby, Age 8, 207
Ramona the Brave, 207
Reading, 103
Rebound Caper, 460
Relatives Came, The, 115
Remembering Box, The, 208
Representing Superdoll, 547
Resettling, The, 512
Reunion, The, 512
Revenge of the Incredible Dr.
    Rancid and His Youthful
    Assistant, Jeffrey, 213
Rhinehart Lifts, 508
Rickshaw to Horror, 109
Rifka Grows Up, 195
Ring of Endless Light, 511
Roadside Valentine, 394
Rocking Chair Rebellion,
    The, 440
Roll of Thunder, Hear My
    Cry, 580
Ronia, the Robber's
    Daughter, 268

Room Made of Windows, A, 430
Rosa Parks, 353
Rose Blanche, 249
Rosie and Michael, 141
Rosie's Razzle Dazzle
    Deal, 240
Ruby!, 5
Runaway Voyage, 431
Running With Rachel, 329
Ruth Marini: Dodger Ace, 432
Ruth Marini of the Dodgers, 432
Ruth Marini World Series, 432

S

Sadako and the Thousand Paper
    Cranes, 335
Sally Ann Thunder Ann Whirlwind
    Crockett, 33
Sally Ride and the New
    Astronauts, 372
Salted Lemons, 309
Samson Svenson's Baby, 95
Sanctuary Tree, The, 503
Sara Crewe, or What Happened at
    Miss Minchin's, 194
Sarah, Plain and Tall, 274
Sasha: The Life of Alexandra
    Tolstoy, 659
Say Hello, Vanessa, 120
Sea Glass, 600
Sea Rovers, The: Pirates,
    Privateers, and Buccaneers, 648
Seafaring Women, 616
Secret Grove, 212
Secret Selves, 400
Secret Soldier, The, 367
Self Portrait: Margo Zemach, 392
Self Portrait: Trina Schart
    Hyman, 359
Seven Daughters and Seven
    Sons, 442
Seven Ravens, The, 56
Shoeshine Girl, 192
Sidney Rella and the Glass
    Sneaker, 279
Sick Day, The, 88
Silas and Con, 311

Silver On the Tree, 451
Single Speckled Egg, A, 82
Sirens and Spies, 579
Skitterbrain, 191
Skystars: The History of Women
    in Aviation, 635
Sleeping, 103
Softball for Girls and Women, 650
Someday With My Father, 20
Something Is Wrong at My
    House, 36
Something Queer Is Going On, 83
Something to Shout About, 184
Song of the Trees, 580
Soonie and the Dragon, 285
Sorrow's Song, 200
South Star, 242
Special Gift, The, 306
Spirit on the Wall, 473
Spirit to Ride the Wild
    Wind, A, 514
Stairway to Doom, 109
Star for the Latecomer, A, 601
Stones, The, 489
Stories for Free Children, 297
Story for a Black Night, 410
Strange Enchantment, A, 397
Strictly for Laughs, 447
String in the Harp, A, 418
Stubborn Old Woman, The, 21
Summer I Learned About
    Life, The, 530
Summer of My German
    Soldier, 476
Summer of the Burning, 459
Summer of the Stallion, 486
Summer to Die, A, 515
Susan B. Anthony, 612
Susannah and the Blue House
    Mystery, 220
Sweet Whispers, Brother
    Rush, 485
Sweetly Sings the Donkey, 435
Sybil Rides for
    Independence, 190

T

Taildraggers High, 577
Taking Care of Melvin, 121
Tangle of Roots, A, 475
Taste of Daylight, A, 583
Tattie's River Journey, 98
Team, The, 550
Ten, Nine, Eight, 11
Terrible Thing That Happened at Our House, The, 17
Tex, 492
That Julia Redfern, 430
That's One Ornery Orphan, 405
Third Eye, The, 497
Those Wonderful Women in Their Flying Machines, 639
Three and Many Wishes of Jason Reid, The, 248
Three Days on a River in a Red Canoe, 146
Three Wishes, 31
Through Grandpa's Eyes, 275
Thunder at Gettysburg, 227
Tilly's House, 70
Time of Hunting, A, 458
Time To Be Brave, A, 259
Time to Get Out of the Bath, Shirley, 22
Tin Can Tucker, 481
Tina Gogo, 401
To Spoil the Sun, 559
To the End of the Block, 100
Toad on Capitol Hill, The, 188
Toby Alone, 421
Toby and Johnny Joe, 421
Toby, Granny, and George, 421
Toliver's Secret, 189
Tomboy, 257
Tough Tiffany, 499
Travellers by Night, 171
The Trek, 73
Trial Valley, 438
Trouble With Dragons, 303
Trouble With Princesses, The, 239
Trouble With Thirteen, The, 531
Trouble's Child, 593
Tryouts, The, 267

Tuck Everlasting, 178
Tucker and the Horse Thief, 314
Tuppeny, 455
Turn Homeward Hannalee, 406
Two of Them, The, 7
Two That Were Tough, 193
Two Young Dancers: Their World of Ballet, 611

U

Under the Early Morning Trees, 4
Up and Up, 65
Up in Seth's Room, 528

V

Very Young Rider, A, 362
Very Young Skater, A, 363
View Beyond My Father, The, 398
Visiting Pamela, 76

W

Walk My Way, 457
Walk on a Snowy Night, A, 37
Walk When the Moon is Full, 237
War Comes to Willy Freeman, 443
War on Villa Street, The, 526
Washday, 94
Watch the Stars Come Out, 81
We Are Mesquakie, We Are One, 251
We Dare Not Go A-Hunting, 516
We Remember Philip, 307
We, the American Women: A Documentary History, 651
Westing Game, The, 556
Westmark, 395
Westward the Women, 553
What About Annie?, 533
What About Grandma?, 500
What Can She Be? A Computer Scientist, 346
What Can She Be? A Farmer, 347
What Can She Be? A Film Producer, 348

What Can She Be? A
  Geologist, 349
What Can She Be? A
  Legislator, 350
What Does the Rooster Say,
  Yoshio?, 13
What Happened To Mr.
  Forster, 403
What's an Average Kid Like Me
  Doing Way Up Here?, 301
When Batistine Made Bread, 84
When I'm Sleepy, 63
When the Boys Ran the
  House, 204
When the Phone Rang, 527
When the Rattlesnake Sounds:
  A Play, 434
When We Went to the Park, 66
Where to Now, Blue?, 312
White House Autumn, 595
Who Is a Stranger and What
  Should I Do?, 155
Who Is Carrie?, 444
Who Kidnapped the Sheriff? Tales
  from Tickfaw, 201
Who's Going to Clean Up the
  Mess?, 260
Why Am I So Miserable If
  These Are the Best Years
  of My Life?, 618
Why Me?, 448
Why Me? Help for Victims of
  Sexual Abuse (Even If They're
  Adults Now), 614
Wild Animals, Gentle
  Women, 621
Wild Horse Killers, The, 463
Wild Robin, 71
Wild Swans, The, 174
Wild Washerwomen, The: A New
  Folk Tale, 148
William, 496
Windows of Elissa, The, 557
Winners, 445
Winners: Women and the Nobel
  Prize, 667
Witch of Port Lajoye, The, 404

Wizard in the Tree, The, 172
Wolf of Shadows, 576
Woman Against Slavery, 662
Woman Chief, 378
Woman in the Moon and
  Other Tales of Forgotten
  Heroines, 558
Woman Power in Textile and
  Apparel Sales, 666
Women Astronauts: Aboard the
  Shuttle, 622
Women at Their Work, 338
Women in Policing: Fighting
  Crime Around the World, 340
Women in Science, 629
Women in Sports: Horseback
  Riding, 345
Women Lawyers at Work, 677
Women Pioneers of
  Science, 631
Women Who Made the West,
  The, 680
Women Who Work With
  Animals, 354
Wonderwomen of Sports, 361
Words By Heart, 567
World of Sports for Girls, A, 653
Worldstone, 575

Y
Yentl, the Yeshiva Boy, 568
Yesterday's Horses, 218
You Can't Be Timid With a
  Trumpet, 619
You Think It's Fun to Be
  a Clown, 2
Young Landlords, The, 536
Your Old Pal, Al, 233
You're a Real Hero,
  Amanda, 323
Yours Till Niagara Falls, 289

Z
Z for Zachariah, 539
Zan Hagen's Marathon, 509
Zia, 290

FICTION SUBJECT INDEX

(References are to annotation numbers)

ACTING
SEE CREATIVE ASPIRATIONS

ADOLESCENT PROBLEMS
Almost Grown, 578
The Cheerleader, 507
Cute is a Four Letter Word, 549
Dinky Hocker Shoots Smack, 506
First the Egg, 534
The Genessee Queen, 520
Hey Dollface, 487
I'm Not Your Other Half, 450
The Liberation of Tansy
    Warner, 585
A Little Love, 483
Marathon Miranda, 325
Megan's Beat, 572
Rebound Caper, 460
Representing Superdoll, 547
The Ring of Endless Light, 511
Roadside Valentine, 394
Tex, 492
The Trouble with Thirteen, 531
Up in Seth's Room, 528
The War on Villa Street, 526
Why Me?, 448

ADVENTURE
After Pa Was Shot, 173
Come Away From the Water,
    Shirley, 22
Courage to Adventure, 205
Fly Into Danger, 552
Ghost Island, 263
In the Face of Danger, 254
In the Shadow of the Bear, 562
Master Rosalind, 407
Night Cry, 286
Nobody Else Can Walk It for
    You, 548
Sara Crewe, 194
Tattie's River Journey, 98
Three Days on the River in a Red
    Canoe, 146
Who Kidnapped the Sheriff? Tales
    from Tickfaw, 201
Wild Horse Killers, 463

AFRICAN LIFE & CULTURE
Bimwili and the Zimwi: A Tale
    from Zanzibar, 1
Comfort Herself, 255
Story for a Black Night, 410

AIRPLANES
Chase the Sun, 532
The Summer I Learned About
    Life, 530
Taildraggers High, 577

ALCOHOLISM
Walk My Way, 457
The War on Villa Street, 526

AMERICA

COLONIAL PERIOD:
Becky and the Bear, 139
A Parcel of Patterns, 592
Rachel and Obadiah, 136

REVOLUTIONARY PERIOD:
Danbury's Burning!, 53
Phoebe and the General, 236
The Summer of the Burning, 459
Sybil Rides for
    Independence, 190
Toliver's Secret, 189
War Comes to Willy
    Freeman, 443
Who is Carrie?, 444

CIVIL WAR/
WAR BETWEEN THE STATES:
Thunder at Gettysburg, 227
Turn Homeward, Hannalee, 406

WAR OF 1812:
The Toad on Capitol Hill, 188

NINETEENTH CENTURY:
After Pa Was Shot, 173
The Bargain Bride, 262
Before the Lark, 427
Beyond the Divide, 510
By Crumbs, It's Mine, 182
Carlota, 540
The Day of the Blizzard, 284
A Gathering of Days, 413
Just Some Weeds in the
    Wilderness, 183
The Liberation of Clementine
    Tipton, 224
Orphan Train, 521
The Runaway Voyage, 431
Something to Shout About, 184
A Spirit to Ride the Wild
    Wind, 514
That's One Ornery Orphan, 405
Words By Heart, 567

TWENTIETH CENTURY:
All Together Now, 423
The Best Bad Thing, 588
Billy Bedamned, Long Gone
    By, 181
The Fragile Flag, 264
The Happiest Ending, 588
Ike & Mama and the Once-A-Year
    Suit, 128
Kentucky Daughter, 565
Toby Trilogy, 421
Zia, 290

DEPRESSION, 1930'S:
Dark Didn't Catch Me
    Trilogy, 583
Julie's Summer, 583
Let the Circle Be Unbroken
    Trilogy, 580
A Taste of Daylight, 583
What About Annie?, 533
You're a Real Hero, Amanda, 323

WORLD WAR II, 1940'S:
Salted Lemons, 309
The Stones, 489

Summer of My German
    Soldier, 476

**AMERICAN/CANADIAN
INDIAN LIFE & CULTURE**
Buffalo Woman, 501
Dancing Feathers, 258
The Goat in the Rug, 19
Good Stones, 464
Homeward the Arrow's Flight, 428
The Hungry Woman: Myths of
    the Aztecs, 412
Legend Days, 490
The Legend of Bluebonnet, 39
Mouse Woman and the Vanished
    Princess, 238
A Time to Be Brave, 259
To Spoil the Sun, 550
The Trouble with
    Princesses, 239
We are Mesquakie, We
    are One, 251
Winners, 445
The Witch of Port
    Lajoye, 404
Zia, 290

ANCIENT TIMES
Four Horses for Tishtray, 598
The Windows of Elissa, 557

ANIMAL STORIES
Cable Car to Catastrophe, 109
A Country Tale, 131
Edgemont, 119
Emma's Pet, 89
Ernest & Celestine Books, 140
Express Train to Trouble, 109
First Snow, 86
Forecast, 58
Hazel's Amazing Mother, 144
I Am a Big Help, 106
Jerome the Babysitter, 29
Liza Lou and the Yeller Belly
    Swamp, 93
Louanne Pig Stories, 26
Millicent the Magnificent, 9

Naughty Nancy Goes to
    School, 51
Pearl's Promise, 177
Rickshaw to Horror, 109
Say Hello, Vanessa, 120
Stairway to Doom, 109
Taking Care of Melvin, 121

APPALACHIA
Come Sing, Jimmy Jo, 543

AUNTS
The Get-Away Car, 209
The House in Norham
    Gardens, 513
The Hundred Penny Box, 276
Just Us Women, 24
Peppermints in the Parlor, 322
Zia, 290

AUSTRALIA
The Hammerhead Light, 315
Playing Beatie Bow, 542

BABIES
Baby and I Can Play, 59
A Baby for Max, 158
Dad's Book books, 103
Fun With Toddlers, 59
Good Wife, Good Wife, 42
Great Grandfather, the Baby and
    Me, 77
I Love My Baby Sister (Most of the
    Time), 44
I Want To Tell You About My
    Baby, 12
My Mama Needs Me, 143
101 Things to Do With a Baby, 104

BABY SITTING
George the Babysitter, 64
Jerome the Babysitter, 29
My Own Private Sky, 408

BALLOONISTS
The Big Balloon Race, 32

BEDTIME
Sleeping, 103
Ten, Nine, Eight, 11
When I'm Sleepy, 63

THE BLACK EXPERIENCE
Arilla Sundown, 482
Big Sister Tells Me I'm
    Black, 3
Black Sister, 677
Breadsticks and Blessing
    Places, 419
Children of the Sun, 581
Daddy, 23
Daddy is a Monster...
    Sometimes, 133
Darlene, 54
A Girl Called Bob and a Horse
    Called Yoki, 203
A Girl Called Boy, 498
Just Us Women, 24
The Hundred Penny Box, 276
Let the Circle Be Unbroken, 580
Listen for the Fig Tree, 524
A Little Love, 483
Ludell Series, 597
M.C. Higgins the Great, 484
Marked by Fire, 582
My Daddy Don't Go to Work, 101
Phoebe and the General, 236
Roll of Thunder, Hear My
    Cry, 580
Song of the Trees, 580
Sweet Whispers, Brother
    Rush, 485
Tough Tiffany, 499
Trouble's Child, 593
War Comes to Willy
    Freeman, 443
When the Rattlesnake
    Sounds, 434
Words By Heart, 567

BOYS

ATHLETIC:
Littlest Leaguer, 62

Rebound Caper, 460
Rinehart Lifts, 508

MUSICAL, DANCERS:
Ben's Trumpet, 68
Doug Meets the
    Nutcracker, 243
Max, 69
A Special Gift, 306

SENSITIVE, NONCONFORMIST:
Accident, 27
Anna Banana & Me, 18
Arthur's Honey Bear, 61
A Bundle of Sticks, 277
The Cheerleader, 507
Danza, 478
Fishman & Charly, 456
Half Nelson, Full Nelson, 573
Left-Handed Shortstop, 229
Like Jake & Me, 74
Much Ado About Aldo, 246
Oliver Button is a Sissy, 41
The Once-In-A-While Hero, 169
Part-Time Boy, 180
Revenge of the Incredible Dr.
    Rancid and His Youthful
    Assistant, Jeffrey, 213
A Time of Hunting, 458

BROTHERS
SEE ALSO BABIES
Goodbye, Arnold!, 300
Millicent the Magnificent, 9
Tex, 492
When the Boys Ran the
    House, 204

BROTHERS AND SISTERS
Bad Dreams of a Good Girl, 304
Betsy & the Chicken Pox, 147
Chinwe, 429
Dicey's Song, 589
The Ghost-Eye Tree, 91
Great Grandfather, the Baby,
    & Me, 77
The Half-Birthday Party, 107

Homecoming, 589
Journey of the Shadow Bairns, 175
Lizzie's Floating Shop, 591
Nadia the Willful, 6
Nobody's Family is Going to
    Change, 467
Pearl in the Egg, 319
Rachel & Obadiah, 136
Rosie's Razzle Dazzle Deal, 240
Watch the Stars Come Out, 81
When the Phone Rang, 527
Wild Robin, 71

BUSINESS VENTURES
Anywhere Else But Here, 439
By Crumbs, It's Mine, 182
Captain Morgana Mason, 471
The Golden Venture, 223
Just Some Weeds in the
    Wilderness, 183
Lizzie's Floating Shop, 591
Luck of Texas McCoy, 529
The Mariah Delaney Lending
    Library, 235
Rachel's Legacy, 446
The Young Landlords, 536

CAMPING
Ghost Island, 263
In the Shadow of the Bear, 562
Katy Did It, 187
Nobody Else Can Walk It for
    You, 548
Yours Til Niagara Falls, 289

CANADA
The Dancing Sun, 176
A Northern Nativity, 261
One Proud Summer, 488
A Time to Be Brave, 259
The Witch of Port Lajoye, 404

CAREERS
M.V. Sexton Speaking, 538
Ruby!, 5
The Summer I Learned About
    Life, 530

CATS
A Country Tale, 131

CHILDHOOD FEARS & FRUSTRATIONS
First Snow, 86
The Ghost-Eye Tree, 91
Goodbye, Arnold!, 300
Hand-Me-Down Kid, 293
Home Alone!, 117
Jim Meets the Thing, 34
Like Jake & Me, 74
My Mama Needs Me, 143
My Own Private Sky, 408
Night Cry, 286
Visiting Pamela, 70
Yours Til Niagara Falls, 289

CHINESE LIFE
Child of the Owl, 599
Sea Glass, 600

CHRISTMAS
All Those Mothers at the
    Manger, 46
Madeline's Christmas, 16
Merry Christmas, Ernest &
    Celestine, 140
Mrs. Claus's Crazy Christmas, 78
A Northern Nativity, 261

THE CIRCUS
Millicent the Magnificent, 9
Travelers by Night, 171

CITY LIFE
Ludell's New York Time, 597
The Young Landlords, 536

CLOWNS
You Think It's Fun to be a Clown, 2

COUNTING BOOKS
Ten, Nine, Eight, 11
When We Went to the Park, 66

COUNTRY & FARM LIFE
Before the Lark, 427
Eliza Pinckney, 160
Euphonia & the Flood, 25
Farm Morning, 90
Guess Who My Favorite Person
    Is, 15
Hazel Rye, 436
Megan's Beat, 572
Sorrow's Song, 200
A Strange Enchantment, 397
Tattie's River Journey, 98
Toby books, 421
Trial Valley, 438
When Batistine Made
    Bread, 84

CREATIVE ASPIRATIONS

ACTING:
Master Rosalind, 407
Oliver Button Is a Sissy, 39

BALLET:
Doug Meets the Nutcracker, 243
Max, 69
Nobody's Family is Going to
    Change, 407
A Special Gift, 306

COMEDY:
Strictly for Laughs, 447

MUSIC:
Ben's Trumpet, 68
Come Sing, Jimmy Jo, 543
Hey Didi Darling, 504
Miranda, 137
Pearl in the Egg, 319

PAINTING, DRAWING:
Emma, 75
In Summer Light, 541
Spirit on the Wall, 473

WRITING:
Arilla Sundown, 482

Keeping Days books, 503
Ruby!, 5

DEATH
Beat the Turtle Drum, 234
Julie's Daughter, 561
Only Love, 563
Ring of Endless Light, 511
A Star for the Latecomer, 601
A Summer to Die, 515
William, 496

DISABILITIES

BLINDNESS
Through Grandpa's Eyes, 275
The View Beyond My Father, 398
Winners, 445

DEAFNESS:
The Mermaid's Three
  Wisdoms, 326

MENTAL HANDICAPS:
The Alfred Summer, 570
Just One Friend, 480

WHEELCHAIR BOUND:
The Balancing Girl, 110
Darlene, 54
Only Love, 563
Rachel, 45

DIVORCE
The Genessee Queen, 520
Getting On With It, 571
My Mother Is Not Married to My
  Father, 291

DOGS
The Accident, 27
The Foundling, 27

DOMESTIC VIOLENCE
Cracker Jackson, 196
Something Is Wrong at My
  House, 36

ENGLAND

16TH CENTURY:
Long Meg, 283
Master Rosalind, 407

17TH CENTURY:
Kate Crackernuts, 424

19TH CENTURY:
Ask Me No Questions, 564
The Mills Down Below, 396

WORLD WAR II:
Home Before Long, 230
A Strange Enchantment, 397

CONTEMPORARY:
Absolute Zero, 453
The Bagthorpe books, 453
The Case of the Baker
  Street Irregulars, 287
Country of Broken
  Stones, 416
Fox in Winter, 420
From Where I Stand, 554
House in Norham
  Gardens, 513
On the Edge, 454
Ordinary Jack, 453

FAIRY TALES
Anna & the Seven Swans, 123
Beauty, 517
The Dancing Sun, 176
The Grey Lady & the
  Strawberry Snatcher, 10
The Paperbag Princess, 96
The Seven Ravens, 56
Sidney Rella and the Glass
  Sneaker, 279
Soonie and the Dragon, 285
A Strange Enchantment, 397
The Trouble With Dragons, 303
Wild Robin, 71
The Wild Swans, 174

FAMILY LIFE

All Kinds of Families, 166
Answer Me, Answer Me, 426
Arilla Sundown, 482
Autumn Street, 271
Bagthorpe saga, 453
Benny Bakes a Cake, 112
Billy Bedamned, Long Gone
    By, 181
By Crumbs It's Mine, 182
Call Me Danica, 519
Captain Morgana Mason, 471
A Chair for My Mother, 145
The Clearance, 512
Come Spring, 472
Country of Broken Stones, 416
The Dark Didn't Catch Me, 583
Dinky Hocker Shoots
    Smack, 506
Don't Forget Michael, 317
Faithfully, Tru, 402
The Faraway Island, 215
First Snow, 86
Glory in the Flower, 503
Goodbye Chicken Little, 197
The Great Skinner Strike, 584
Half Nelson, Full Nelson, 573
Harry's Mom, 108
Homecoming, 589
I Am a Big Help, 106
I'm Busy Too, 124
Just Some Weeds in the
    Wilderness, 183
The Keeping Days, 503
Kentucky Daughter, 565
A Mustard Seed of Magic, 503
The Night Swimmers, 198
Nobody's Family Is Going to
    Change, 467
Of Love, Death & Other
    Journeys, 493
The Pilgrimage, 512
Ramona books, 207
The Relatives Came, 115
The Resettling, 512
The Reunion, 512
The Sanctuary Tree, 503
Sweet Whispers, Brother
    Rush, 485
Sweetly Sings the Donkey, 435
Toby books, 421
Washday, 94
When the Boys Ran the
    House, 204
Where to Now, Blue?, 312
Who's Going to Clean Up the
    Mess?, 260
William, 496

FANTASY

Alanna: The First Adventure, 296
Alexandra the Rock Eater, 138
The Dark is Rising books, 451
The Great Pete Penney, 318
Heraclea: A Legend of Women
    Warriors, 466
The Hero & the Crown, 518
Home, 242
The House in Norham
    Gardens, 513
The Horsemaster, 569
Into the Painted Bear Lair, 310
Jackaroo, 590
Kate Crackernuts, 424
The Looking Glass Factor, 231
Madeline's Christmas, 16
The Magic Porridge Pot, 48
Mermaid's Three Wisdoms, 326
Mrs. Claus's Crazy
    Christmas, 78
Mrs. Gaddy books, 47
Mrs. Minetta's Car Pool, 129
A Necklace of Fallen Stars, 491
A Net to Catch the Wind, 232
Pearl's Promise, 177
Playing Beatie Bow, 542
Princess of Chameln, 596
The Queen & Rosie
    Randall, 292
The Queen's Nose, 256
Ronia the Robber's
    Daughter, 268
Soonie & the Dragon, 285
A String in the Harp, 418

The Three & Many Wishes
  of Jason Reid, 248
The Trek, 73
Tuck Everlasting, 178
Tuppenny, 455
Up & Up, 65
Wesmark Trilogy, 395
Worldstone, 575

FATHERS
Dad's Back, 103
Daddy is a Monster...
  Sometimes, 133
Fishman & Charly, 456
The Girl Who Had No
  Name, 298
I Want to Tell You About
  My Baby, 12
Messy Baby, 103
Nobody's Family is Going to
  Change, 467
Reading, 103
Sleeping, 103

FATHERS & DAUGHTERS
Amy Goes Fishing, 92
Anywhere Else But Here, 439
Carlota, 540
Daddy, 23
Eat Your Peas, Louise!, 127
Elizabeth Catches a Fish, 135
Emma's Pet, 89
Farm Morning, 90
In Summer Light, 541
In the Shadow of the Bear, 562
Isis Pedlar, 495
Katy Did It, 187
My Daddy Don't Go to Work, 101
Nadia the Willful, 6
Of Love, Death & Other
  Journeys, 493
The Sick Day, 88
Someday With My Father, 20
Ten, Nine, Eight, 11
To the End of the Block, 100
Two That Were Tough, 193
A Walk on a Snowy Night, 40

FATHERS & SONS
Daddy & Ben Together, 132
Johnny Castleseed, 105

FEELINGS & EMOTIONS
Bad Dreams of a Good Girl, 304
Country of Broken Stone, 416
Feeling Mad, Feeling Sad, Feeling
  Bad, Feeling Glad, 87
Feelings, 97
Much Ado about Aldo, 246

FEMINISM
Casey & the Great Idea, 288
The Girl With Spunk, 302
Mother, Aunt Susan and Me, 252
Tomboy, 257

FINANCIAL INDEPENDENCE
M.V. Sexton Speaking, 538

FOLK TALES
Bimwili & the Zimwi, 1
Clever Gretchen, 272
The Girl Who Wouldn't Get
  Married, 57
Good Wife, Good Wife, 42
Halfway Up the Mountain, 49
Heraclea, 466
The Hungry Woman, 412
Legend Days, 490
Legend of Bluebonnet, 37
My Mother Sends Her
  Wisdom, 85
Sally Ann Thunder Ann
  Whirlwind Crockett, 33
Seven Daughters & Seven
  Sons, 442
A Single Speckled Egg, 82
The Wild Washerwoman, 148
The Woman in the Moon, 558

FOSTER CARE
The Boy Who Wanted A
  Family, 52
Fox Farm, 219
The Great Gilley Hopkins, 295

The Pinballs, 199
Silas & Con, 311
Tina Gogo, 401

FRIENDSHIP

BETWEEN BOYS:
Benny, 211
Big Man & the Burnout, 409
The Secret Grove, 212

BETWEEN BOYS AND GIRLS:
Al (exandra) the Great, 233
Alfred Summer, 570
All It Takes Is Practice, 281
Anastasia Morningstar & the
    Crystal Butterfly, 247
Anna Banana & Me, 18
Ernest & Celestine books, 140
Everett Anderson's Friend, 30
Friends, 67
A Girl Called Bob and a Horse
    Called Yoki, 203
Let Me Hear the Music, 179
Magic of the Glits, 168
My Friend William Moved
    Away, 60
New Neighbors for Nora, 244
Part Time Boy, 180
A Place to Come Back To, 417
Rinehart Lifts, 508
Rosie & Michael, 141
Three Wishes, 31
What Does the Rooster Say,
    Yoshio?, 13

BETWEEN CHILDREN
& ADULTS:
Anastasia Morningstar & the
    Crystal Butterfly, 247
Bus Ride, 72
Dudley and the Birdman, 313
Guess Who My Favorite Person
    Is?, 15
Just Us Women, 24
Kidnapping of Mr. Huey, 461
The Lilith Summer, 250

Miss Maggie, 114
Mrs. Fish, Ape, and Me, the Dump
    Queen, 278
New Neighbors for Nora, 244

BETWEEN GIRLS:
Between Friends, 225
An End to Perfect, 537
Hammerhead Light, 315
Marathon Miranda, 325
Something Queer is Going On, 83
Visiting Pamela, 76

FRONTIER & PIONEER STORIES
All This Wild Land, 206
Bargain Bride, 262
Beyond the Divide, 510
Orphan Train, 521
Prairie Song, 449
Runaway Voyage, 431
Sarah, Plain and Tall, 274
Skitterbrain, 191
Something to Shout About, 184
Tucker & the Horse Thief, 314
Westward the Women, 553

GERMAN STORIES
In the Face of Danger, 254
Oma, 241
Rose Blanche, 249

GIRLS

ADVENTUROUS:
Anna, Grandpa & the Big
    Storm, 134
Answer Me, Answer Me, 426
Becky & the Bear, 139
The Best of Enemies, 415
The Big Balloon Race, 32
Bimwili & the Zimwi, 1
Danbury's Burning!, 53
Doris Fein, 411
Euphonia & the Flood, 25
Hadder MacColl, 202

Liza Lou & the Yeller Belly
  Swamp, 93
Paperbag Princess, 96
Pearl in the Egg, 319
Runaway Voyage, 431
Sybil Rides for
  Independence, 190
Tattie's River Journey, 98
Wild Horse Killers, 463

ATHLETIC:
The Colonel & Me, 433
Everett Anderson's Friend, 30
First Serve, 586
Hockey Girls, 214
I Am the Running Girl, 170
"Me & You & a Dog Named
  Blue", 452
Ruth Marini books, 432
Tin Can Tucker, 481
The Tryouts, 267
Zan Hagen's Marathon, 509

NONCONFORMIST:
Alexandra the Rock Eater, 138
Anastasia books, 270
The Balancing Girl, 110
Beauty, 517
Busybody Nora, 244
Comfort Herself, 255
Day of the Blizzard, 284
Dusty, 79
The Fragile Flag, 264
The General, 221
The Golden Venture, 223
Hazel Rye, 436
Hand-Me-Down Kid, 293
Handles, 523
Hester the Jester, 122
Homeward the Arrow's
  Flight, 428
The Island Keeper, 525
Long Meg, 283
The Luckie Star, 321
Lucy Mastermind, 222
Mariah Delaney Lending
  Library, 235

My Two Feet, 116
Mrs. Fish, Ape, and Me, the
  Dump Queen, 278
Nadia the Willful, 6
Rifka Grows Up, 195
Ronia the Robber's
  Daughter, 268
Ruby!, 5
Seven Daughters and Seven
  Sons, 442
Shoeshine Girl, 192
Something Queer is Going
  On, 83
Stubborn Old Woman, 21
Tales from Tickfaw, 201
Tomboy, 257
Where to Now, Blue?, 312

GRANDFATHERS
Anna, Grandpa & the Big
  Storm, 134
Good As New, 43
Great-Grandfather, the Baby
  & Me, 77
Hugo & the Princess Nena, 462
Now One Foot, Now the
  Other, 40
Summer of the Stallion, 486
Through Grandpa's Eyes, 275
The Two of Them, 7
When We Went to the Park, 66
Winners, 445

GRANDMOTHERS
Autumn Street, 271
Dodo Every Day, 142
The Dream Keeper, 465
The Faraway Island, 215
The Get-Away Car, 209
Grandma is Somebody Special, 50
Grandmamma's Joy, 55
The Great Pistachio Case, 266
Mandy's Grandmother, 125
My Island Grandma, 80
Oma, 241
Queen of Hearts, 437
The Remembering Box, 208

Toby, Granny & George, 421
What About Grandma?, 500

GRIEF
The Accident, 27
Breadsticks & Blessing
    Places, 419
Bridge to Terabithia, 294
A Fine Soft Day, 470
Fishman & Charly, 456
The Foundling, 27
Magic of the Glits, 168
A Morgan for Melinda, 226
Nadia the Willful, 6
A Place to Come Back To, 417
Ring of Endless Light, 511
A Star for the Latecomer, 601
A Summer to Die, 515
A Tangle of Roots, 475
We Remember Philip, 307
William, 496

HOLLAND
The Stubborn Old Woman, 21

HOMOSEXUALITY
What Happened to Mr.
    Forster, 403

HORSES
The Colonel & Me, 433
The Crumb, 217
Danza!, 478
Flowers of Anger, 479
A Girl Called Bob and a Horse
    Called Yoki, 203
A Morgan for Melinda, 226
Summer of the Stallion, 486
The Team, 550
The Wild Horse Killers, 463
Yesterday's Horses, 218

HOSPITAL
It Can't Hurt Forever, 308

ILLNESS
Betsy & the Chicken Pox, 147

The Sick Day, 88
Someday With My Father, 20
Story for a Black Night, 410

IMMIGRATION
All this Wild Land, 206
Call Me Danica, 519
Dream Keeper, 465
From Where I Stand, 554
Journey of the Shadow
    Bairns, 175
Night Journey, 265
Rachel's Legacy, 446
Watch the Stars Come Out, 81

IRELAND
A Fine Soft Day, 470
The Gift of the Pirate Queen, 228

JAPANESE
The Best Bad Thing, 588
The Eternal Spring of Mr. Ito, 474
Happiest Ending, 588
Jar of Dreams, 588
What Does the Rooster Say,
    Yoshio?, 13

JEWISH LIFE & CULTURE
Benny, 211
Bitter Herbs & Honey, 441
The Night Journey, 265
Rachel's Legacy, 446
The Remembering Box, 208
Rifka Grows Up, 195
The Secret Grove, 212
Summer of My German
    Soldier, 476
Yentl the Yeshiva Boy, 568

LATCH KEY CHILDREN
The Best Mom in the World, 41
Everett Anderson's Friend, 30
Home Alone, 117

**MEN IN NON-
TRADITIONAL ROLES**
Dad's Back, 103

George the Babysitter, 64
Jerome the Babysitter, 29
Messy Baby, 103
Samson Svenson's Baby, 95
Washday, 94

MOTHERS
After Pa Was Shot, 173
The Big Balloon Race, 32
Billy, Bedamned, Long Gone
   By, 181
A Chair for My Mother, 145
Fog Drift Morning, 111
Harry's Mom, 108
Hazel's Amazing Mother, 144
Ike and Mama and the Once-
   A-Year Suit, 128
IOUs, 566
Journey to Almost There, 477
Julie's Daughter, 561
Law of Gravity, 245
Liberation of Tansy
   Warner, 585
My Mama Needs Me, 143
My Mother is the Smartest
   Woman in the World, 210
President's Daughter, 595
A Star for the Latecomer, 601
Three Days on a River
   in a Red Canoe, 146
Whitehouse Autumn, 595
William, 496

MOTHERS WHO WORK
Best Mom in the World, 41
But What About Me?, 269
The Great Skinner Strike, 584
Home Alone, 117
My Mom Got a Job, 126
My Mom Travels a Lot, 14
The Terrible Thing That
   Happened at Our House, 17

MOVING TO A
NEW HOUSE
Come Spring, 472
Grandmamma's Joy, 55

Ludell's New York Time, 597
Sea Glass, 600

MYSTERY AND SUSPENSE
Answer Me, Answer Me, 426
Cable Car to Catastrophe
   books, 109
Case of the Baker Street
   Irregulars, 287
The Crumb, 217
Dangerous Beat, 468
Doris Fein: Superspy, 411
Figure in the Shadows, 186
French Detection, 320
Gabriel's Girl, 502
Girl Who Had No Name, 298
The Great Pistachio Case, 266
Halloween Pumpkin Smasher, 130
The Letter the Witch & the
   Ring, 186
On the Edge, 454
Peppermints in the Parlor, 322
P.J. Clover, Private Eye, 280
Something Queer is Going On, 83
Susannah & the Blue House
   Mystery, 220
We Dare Not Go A-Hunting, 516
The Westing Game, 556

NATURE & ECOLOGY
Dudley & the Birdman, 313
Fishman & Charly, 456
Fly Into Danger, 552
Fog Drift Morning, 111
Ghosts I Have Been, 546
The Island Keeper, 525
M.C. Higgins the Great, 484
Magnum Fault, 560
Quincy's Harvest, 469
Sorrow's Song, 200
Summer of the Stallion, 486
Under the Early Morning
   Trees, 4
Walk When the Moon is
   Full, 237
Wild Horse Killers, 463
Wolf of Shadows, 576

NEW ENGLAND
Becky & the Bear, 139
Best of Enemies, 415
Danbury's Burning, 53
My Island Grandma, 80
A Spirit to Ride the Wild
Wind, 514

OCCULT & SUPERNATURAL
The Changeover, A
Supernatural Romance, 522
Ghost Belonged to Me, 546
Ghosts I Have Been, 546

OLD PEOPLE
Halfway Up the Mountain, 49
Peppermints in the Parlor, 322
Rocking Chair Rebellion, 440

OLD MEN:
Dudley & the Birdman, 313
The Fox in Winter, 420
Kidnapping of Mr. Huey, 461
The Stones, 489
Two That Were Tough, 193
Where to Now, Blue?, 312

OLD WOMEN:
Carrie Hepple's Garden, 35
Emma, 75
Grey Lady & the Strawberry
Snatcher, 10
Lilith Summer, 250
Miss Maggie, 114
Miss Pickerell Takes the
Bull by the Horns, 273
Mrs. Gaddy books, 47
My Own Private Sky, 408
Queen of Hearts, 438
Stubborn Old Woman, 21

ORPHANS
Dicey's Song, 589
Homecoming, 589
Orphan Train, 521
The Orphans, 299

Sara Crewe or What
Happened at Miss
Minchin's, 194
Silas & Con, 311
That's One Ornery Orphan, 405
When the Phone Rang, 527
Winners, 445

PETS
The Accident, 27
The Foundling, 27
The Queen's Nose, 256
A Rabbit for Easter, 28
Samson Svenson's Baby, 95
You're a Real Hero, Amanda, 323

PLAYS
When the Rattlesnake
Sounds, 434

POETRY
All Those Mothers at the
Manger, 46
Almost Grown, 578
Amelia Mixed the Mustard, 99
Big Sister Tells Me I'm Black, 3
Black Sister, 677
Children of the Sun, 501
The Dancing Sun, 176
Free to Be You and Me, 316
Under the Early Morning
Trees, 4

POLITICS/PUBLIC AFFAIRS
The Fragile Flag, 264
Lucy Mastermind, 222
A Matter of Principle, 551
Miss Pickerell Takes the
Bull by the Horns, 273
My Mother is the Smartest
Woman in the World, 210
The President's Daughter, 595
Something to Shout About, 184
What's an Average Kid Like Me
Doing Way Up Here?, 301

POLYNESIAN LIFE
Light in the Mountain, 399

PRE-HISTORY
Maroo of the Winter
  Caves, 587
Spirit on the Wall, 473

PRIMATES
The Gorilla Signs Love, 422

RAPE
Are You in the House
  Alone?, 545
Listen for the Fig Tree, 524
Marked by Fire, 582

ROMANCE
Chase the Sun, 532
I'm Not Your Other Half, 450
A Little Love, 483
Love Match, 555
Secret Selves, 400
Strictly for Laughs, 447
Why Me?, 448

SCHOOLDAYS
First the Egg, 534
Flunking of Joshua T.
  Bates, 305
Jim Meets the Thing, 34
Louanne Pig in the Talent
  Show, 26
Miss Nelson books, 8
Mrs. Peloki's Snake, 102
Naughty Nancy Goes to
  School, 51
What's an Average Kid Like Me
  Doing Way Up Here?, 301

SCIENCE FICTION
Beloved Benjamin is
  Waiting, 253
Changing Times, 505
The Delikon, 494
Green is for Galanx, 574
Isis Pedlar, 495

Looking Glass Factor, 231
Wolf of Shadows, 576
Z for Zachariah, 539

SCOTLAND
The Clearance books, 512
Fox Farm, 219
Hadder MacColl, 202
The Third Eye, 497

SEA STORIES
Chinwe, 429
The Gift of the Pirate
  Queen, 228
Porcelain Pagoda, 535
Runaway Voyage, 431
Watch the Stars Come Out!, 81

SEXUAL ABUSE
A Better Safe Than Sorry
  Book, 156
My Body is Private, 154
Who is a Stranger and What
  Should I Do?, 155

SEXUAL AWAKENING
Hey Dollface, 487
Up in Seth's Room, 528

SHORT STORIES
Courage to Adventure, 205
The Dancing Sun, 176
Free to be You and Me, 316
Stories for Free Children, 297
The Trouble With
  Princesses, 239
Westward the Women, 553
The Woman in the Moon, 558

SHYNESS
Faraway Island, 215
Say Hello, Vanessa, 120

SISTERS
I Love My Baby Sister, 44
Jacob Have I Loved, 544
Sirens and Spies, 579

The Windows of Elissa, 557

SLAVERY AND ABOLITION
Chinwe, 429
The Dancing Sun, 176
Four Horses for Tishtray, 598
A Girl Called Boy, 498
When the Rattlesnake
    Sounds, 434
Who is Carrie?, 444

SPORT STORIES
Amy Goes Fishing, 92
The Cheerleader, 507
Elizabeth Catches a Fish, 135
First Serve, 586
The Great Pete Penney, 318
Hockey Girls, 214
I Am the Running Girl, 170
Left-Handed Shortstop, 229
Littlest Leaguer, 62
Louanne Pig in Making the
    Team, 26
Love Match, 555
Rebound Caper, 460
Rinehart Lifts, 508
Ruth Marini books, 432
The Team, 550
The Tryouts, 267
Zan Hagen's Marathon, 509

STEPPARENTS
Like Jake & Me, 74
Sarah, Plain and Tall, 274

TEACHERS
Maudie & Me & the Dirty
    Book, 282
Miss Nelson books, 8
Mrs. Peloki's Snake, 102
What Happened to Mr.
    Forster, 403

TOYS, BEARS & DOLLS
Arthur's Honey Bear, 61
Good As New, 43

Tilly's House, 70

WALES
A String in the Harp, 418

WAR
Autumn Streets, 271
Conrad's War, 216
The Eternal Spring of Mr. Ito, 474
Home Before Long, 230
The Machine Gunners, 594
Rose Blanche, 249
Sadako & the Thousand Paper
    Cranes, 335
A Strange Enchantment, 397
Summer of My German
    Soldier, 476
The Windows of Elissa, 557

WITCHES & WIZARDS
The Figure in the Shadows, 186
The House With a Clock in its
    Walls, 186
The Letter, the Witch and the
    Ring, 186
Madeline's Christmas, 16
A Necklace of Fallen Stars, 491
The Wizard in the Tree, 172

NON-FICTION SUBJECT INDEX
(References are to annotation numbers)

AMERICA

COLONIAL PERIOD:
Annie Oakley and the World of Her
  Time, 602
Children of the Wild West, 624
Demeter's Daughters, 682

REVOLUTIONARY PERIOD:
Abigail Adams, 159
Founding Mothers, 615
I'm Deborah Sampson, 333
Secret Soldier, 367

NINETEENTH CENTURY:
Mill Girls, 664
Laura Ingalls Wilder, 331
Women Who Made the West, 680

OVERVIEW: PAST TO PRESENT
As I Saw It, 637
Changing Face of the
  Constitution, 642
We, the American Women, 651

AMERICAN INDIAN LIFE AND CULTURE
Chief Sarah, 652
Daisy Hooee Nampeyo, 341
Double Life of Pocahontas, 625
Woman Chief, 378

ANIMALS AND ANIMAL BEHAVIOR
Animal Fathers, 344
Marina and Ruby, 626
Wild Animals, Gentle Women, 621
Women Who Work With
  Animals, 354

ART AND ARTISTS
Breaking Tradition: The Story
  of Louise Nevelson, 606
Daisy Hooee Nampeyo, 341
Drawn from New England:

Tasha Tudor, 383
From the Hills of Georgia: An
  Autobiography in Paintings, 656
New Women in Art and Dance, 608
Self Portrait: Margo Zemach, 392
Self Portrait: Trina Schart
  Hyman, 359

ASTRONAUTS
Sally Ride and the New
  Astronauts, 372
Women Astronauts, 622

ATHLETES
Chris Evert, the Young
  Champion, 632
Famous Women Tennis
  Players, 623
Janet Guthrie: First Woman
  at Indy, 373
Janet Guthrie: Foot to
  the Floor, 342
Martina Navratilova, 364
Mary Lou Retton: A
  Biography, 379
Mary Lou Retton: Gold Medal
  Gymnast, 365
Picture Story of Nancy
  Lopez, 375
Racing Against the Odds, 332
Raising a Racket: Rosie
  Casals, 381
Very Young Rider, 362
Very Young Skater, 363
Women in Sports: Horseback
  Riding, 345
Wonderwomen of Sports, 361

AVIATION
Breakthrough: Women in
  Aviation, 673
Skystars, 635
Those Wonderful Women in
  Their Flying Machines, 639

BABIES
Baby and I Can Play, 59
Baby for Max, 158
Fun With Toddlers, 59
New Baby, 165
New Baby at Your House, 151
Oh Boy! Babies, 357

BIOGRAPHY
Abigail Adams, 159
Alicia Alonzo, 669
All in All: A Biography of
    George Eliot, 627
Annie Oakley and the World
    of her Time, 602
Barbara Jordan: The Great
    Lady from Texas, 164
Before the Supreme Court:
    The Story of Belva Ann
    Lockwood, 617
Bella Abzug, 620
Betty Friedan, 368
Breaking Tradition: The
    Story of Louise Nevelson, 606
Carrie Nation, 647
Chief Sarah, 652
Chris Evert, the Young
    Champion, 632
Coretta Scott King, 374
Dolly Parton: Country Goin'
    to Town, 376
Dorothea Lange: A Life Through
    the Camera, 369
Eleanor Roosevelt: A Life of
    Happiness and Tears, 360
Eliza Pinckney, 160
Equal Justice: A Biography
    of Sandra Day O'Connor, 390
Eye on the World: Margaret
    Bourke-White,
    Photographer, 670
Free Woman: The Life and Times
    of Victoria Woodhull, 649
Frontiers of Dance: The Life
    of Martha Graham, 678
Geraldine Ferraro, 643
Golda Meir Story, 336

I Will Be A Doctor: The
    Story of America's First
    Woman Physician, 387
Indira Gandhi, 613
Jane Goodall, 334
Janet Guthrie: First Woman
    at Indy, 373
Janet Guthrie: Foot to the
    Floor, 342
Joan of Arc, 607
Justice Sandra Day O'Connor, 343
Laura Ingalls Wilder, 331
Lena Horne, 634
Lillian Wald of Henry Street, 671
Margaret Fuller, 683
Margaret Sanger, 679
Martina Navratilova, 364
Mary Lou Retton: A
    Biography, 379
Mary Lou Retton: Gold
    Medal Gymnast, 365
Mary McLeod Bethune, 352
Mother Teresa, 351
Our Golda: The Story of
    Golda Meir, 327
Queen Eleanor: Independent
    Spirit of the Medieval
    World, 609
Queen Elizabeth I, 684
Racing Against the Odds, 332
Rosa Parks, 353
Sasha: The Life of Alexandra
    Tolstoy, 659
Secret Soldier, 367
Susan B. Anthony, 612
Woman Against Slavery, 662
Woman Chief, 378

BLACK EXPERIENCE
Barbara Jordan, 164
Black Sister, 676
Childtimes: A Three
    Generational Memoir, 630
Coretta Scott King, 374
Katherine Dunham, 633
Mary McLeod Bethune, 352
Rosa Parks, 353

BOYS
Boys Have Feelings Too, 610
I Love to Dance, 391
Oh Boy! Babies, 357

CAREER SUGGESTIONS
Fine Trades, 663
I Can Be A Truck Driver, 150
I Want to be a Fisherman, 386
What Can She Be? A Computer
  Scientist, 346
What Can She Be? A Farmer, 347
What Can She Be? A Film
  Producer, 348
What Can She Be? A
  Geologist, 349
What Can She Be? A
  Legislator, 350
Woman Power in Textile and
  Apparel Sales, 666
Women at Their Work, 338
Women Who Work With
  Animals, 354

LATINO LIFE
AND CULTURE
Alicia Alonzo, 669

CHINESE HISTORY
AND SOCIETY
Chinese Women in History
  and Legend, 646

CIVIL RIGHTS MOVEMENT
Coretta Scott King, 374
Rosa Parks, 353

COOKING
Johnny's Egg, 162

DANCE
Alicia Alonzo, 669
Frontiers of Dance: The Life
  of Martha Graham, 678
I Love to Dance, 391
Katherine Dunham, 633

New Women in Art and
  Dance, 608
Two Young Dancers, 611

DAYCARE
Going to Daycare, 165

DISABILITIES
Amy: The Story of a
  Deaf Child, 385
Anna's Silent World, 388
Connie's New Eyes, 389
I Have a Sister—My Sister
  is Deaf, 163

EMOTIONS AND
BEHAVIOR
Boys Have Feelings Too, 610
Feeling Safe Feeling
  Strong, 380
No More Secrets for Me, 384
Options: The Female Teen's
  Guide to Coping With the
  Problems of Today's World, 665
Who is a Stranger and What
  Should I Do?, 155
Why Am I So Miserable if These
  Are the Best Years of My
  Life?, 618
Why Me? Help for Victims of
  Child Sexual Abuse, 614

ENGLISH HISTORY
AND SOCIETY
Queen Eleanor: Independent
  Spirit of the Medieval
  World, 609
Queen Elizabeth I, 684

FAMILIES
All Kinds of Families, 166
Life With Working Parents, 356

FARMING
What Can She Be?
  A Farmer, 347

FEMINISM
Betty Friedan, 368
Flora Tristan, 661
Founding Mothers, 615
Free Woman: The Life and
    Times of Victoria Woodhull, 649
Ladies Were Not Expected, 371
Margaret Fuller, 683
Susan B. Anthony, 612

FIRST LADIES
Abigail Adams, 159
Eleanor Roosevelt: A Life of
    Happiness and Tears, 360

FRENCH LANGUAGE
Let's Go/Allons-Y, 153

GIRLS
Cowgirl, 167
Journey to the Soviet Union, 377
Little Britches Rodeo, 382
Music Lessons for Alex, 328
Sadako and the Thousand Paper
    Cranes, 335
Very Young Rider, 362
Very Young Skater, 363

HEALTH AND MEDICINE
Contributions of Women:
    Medicine, 658
Doctors for the People, 645
Early Morning Rounds, 636
Margaret Sanger, 679
New Women in Medicine, 608

JAPANESE LIFE
AND CULTURE
Sadako and the Thousand Paper
    Cranes, 335

JEWISH LIFE
AND CULTURE
Clara's Story, 638
In the Mouth of the Wolf, 685
Mischling, Second Degree, 641

LABOR MOVEMENT
Labor: Contributions
    of Women, 604
Mill Girls, 664

LAW ENFORCEMENT
Breakthrough: Women in
    Law Enforcement, 673
Women in Policing, 340

LAW AND LAWYERS
Before the Supreme Court:
    The Story of Belva Ann
    Lockwood, 617
Breakthrough: Women in Law, 672
Changing Face of the
    Constitution, 642
Equal Justice: A Biography
    of Sandra Day O'Connor, 390
Justice Sandra Day
    O'Connor, 343
New Women in Politics, 608
What Can She Be? A
    Legislator, 350
Women Lawyers at Work, 677

MEDIA
Breakthrough: Women in
    Television, 672
Hot off the Press, 370
New Women in Media, 608
What Can She Be? A
    Film Producer, 348

MOTHERS WHO WORK
Ask Me What My Mother
    Does, 161
Life With Working Parents, 356
Night Dive, 366

PHOTOGRAPHERS
Dorothea Lange: Life Through
    the Camera, 369
Eye On the World:
    Margaret Bourke-White,
    Photographer, 670

PIONEER WOMEN
Annie Oakley and the World
  of her Time, 602
As I Saw It: Women Who Lived
  the American Adventure, 637
Children of the Wild West, 624
Demeter's Daughters, 682
Women Who Made the West, 680

QUEENS
Catherine the Great, 640
Queen Eleanor: Independent Spirit
  of the Medieval World, 609
Queen Elizabeth I, 684

RODEO
Little Britches Rodeo, 382

SEX ROLES
In Christina's Toolbox, 157
Male/Female Roles, 644

SEXUAL ABUSE
Better Safe Than Sorry Book, 156
Feeling Safe Feeling Strong, 380
My Body Is Private, 154
No More Secrets For Me, 384
Who Is A Stranger and What
  Should I Do?, 155
Why Me? Help for Victims of Child
  Sexual Abuse, 614

SLAVERY AND ABOLITION
Susan B. Anthony, 612
Woman Against Slavery, 662

SOCIAL REFORMERS
Betty Friedan, 368
Carrie Nation, 647
Coretta Scott King, 374
Eleanor Roosevelt: A Life of
  Happiness and Tears, 360
Flora Tristan, 661
Free Woman: The Life and Times
  of Victoria Woodhull, 649
Labor: Contributions of
  Women, 604

Ladies Were Not Expected, 371
Lillian Wald of Henry
  Street, 671
Margaret Sanger, 679
Mother Teresa, 351
Rosa Parks, 353
Sasha: The Life of Alexandra
  Tolstoy, 659
Woman Against Slavery, 662

SPORTS
Annapurna: A Woman's
  Place, 605
Chris Evert, the Young
  Champion, 632
Famous Women Tennis
  Players, 623
I Love Softball, 330
I Skate, 339
Improving Women's
  Running, 675
It's a Girl's Game Too, 668
Junior Weight Training and
  Strength Training, 674
Mary Lou Retton: A
  Biography, 379
Mary Lou Retton: Gold Medal
  Gymnast, 365
Perfect Balance, 355
Racing Against the Odds, 332
Running With Rachel, 329
Softball for Girls and Women, 650
Very Young Rider, A, 362
Very Young Skater, A, 363
World of Sports for Girls, A, 653

WAR
Clara's Story, 638
In the Mouth of the Wolf, 685
Mischling, Second Degree, 641

WOMEN—COLLECTED
BIOGRAPHIES
Breakthrough: Women in
  Archaeology, 681
Breakthrough: Women in
  Aviation, 673

Breakthrough: Women in
 Law, 672
Breakthrough: Women in
 Law Enforcement, 673
Breakthrough: Women in
 Religion, 672
Breakthrough: Women in
 Science, 628
Breakthrough: Women in
 Television, 672
Breakthrough: Women in
 Writing, 628
Contemporary Women Scientists
 of America, 654
Contributions of Women:
 Literature, 655
Contributions of Women:
 Medicine, 658
Contributions of Women:
 Music, 660
Contributions of Women:
 Science, 337
Dreams into Deeds, 657
Famous American Tennis
 Players, 623
New Women in Art and Dance, 608
New Women in
 Entertainment, 608
New Women in Media, 608
New Women in Medicine, 608
New Women in Politics, 608
New Women in Social
 Sciences, 608
One Hundred Greatest Women
 in Sports, 358
Sally Ride and the New
 Astronauts, 372
Skystars, 635
Wild Animals, Gentle Women, 621
Winners: Women and the Nobel
 Prize, 445
Women Astronauts: Aboard the
 Shuttle, 622
Women at Their Work, 338
Women in Science, 629
Women Pioneers of Science, 631
Women Who Made the West, 680

Women Who Work With
 Animals, 354

**WOMEN—DIARIES,
JOURNALS, AND LETTERS**
As I Saw It, 637
Childtimes: A Three Generational
 Memoir, 630
We, The American Women, 651

WOMEN AND FILM
What Can She Be? A Film
 Producer, 348

WOMEN AND HEALTH
Contributions of Women:
 Medicine, 658
Doctors for the People, 645
Early Morning Rounds, 636
I Will Be a Doctor, 387
New Women in Medicine, 608
Margaret Sanger, 679

WOMEN AT SEA
Sea Rovers, 648
Seafaring Women, 616

WOMEN IN BUSINESS
What Can She Be? A
 Computer Scientist, 346

WOMEN IN EDUCATION
Mary McLeod Bethune, 352

**WOMEN IN LAW AND
LAW ENFORCEMENT**
Before the Supreme Court:
 The Story of Belva Ann
 Lockwood, 617
Breakthrough: Women in
 Law, 672
Breakthrough: Women in Law
 Enforcement, 673
Equal Justice: A Biography
 of Sandra Day O'Connor, 390
Justice Sandra Day
 O'Connor, 343

Women in Policing, 340
Women Lawyers at Work, 677

WOMEN IN LITERATURE
All in All: A Biography
  of George Eliot, 627
Black Sister: Poetry by
  Black American Women
  1746-1980, 676
Breakthrough: Women in
  Writing, 628
Contributions of Women:
  Literature, 655
Laura Ingalls Wilder, 331

WOMEN IN MUSIC
Contributions of Women:
  Music, 660
Dolly Parton: Country Goin'
  to Town, 376
Girl Groups, 603
Lena Horne, 634
Music Lessons for Alex, 328
New Women in
  Entertainment, 608
You Can't Be Timid With
  a Trumpet, 619

WOMEN IN POLITICS
Barbara Jordan: The Great Lady
  from Texas, 164
Bella Abzug, 620
Geraldine Ferraro, 643
Golda Meir Story, 336
Indira Gandhi, 613
New Women in Politics, 608
Our Golda: The Story of
  Golda Meir, 327
What Can She Be? A
  Legislator, 350

WOMEN IN RELIGION
Breakthrough: Women in
  Religion, 672
Joan of Arc, 607
Mother Teresa, 351

WOMEN IN SCIENCE
Breakthrough: Women in
  Archaeology, 681
Breakthrough: Women in
  Science, 628
Contemporary Women Scientists
  of America, 654
Contributions of Women:
  Science, 337
Jane Goodall, 334
I Will Be a Doctor, 387
New Women in Social
  Sciences, 608
Night Dive, 366
Sally Ride and the New
  Astronauts, 372
What Can She Be? A
  Geologist, 349
Women Astronauts: Aboard
  the Shuttle, 622
Women in Science, 629
Women Pioneers of Science, 631

WOMEN IN SPORTS
Annapurna: A Woman's
  Place, 605
Chris Evert, the Young
  Champion, 632
Famous Women Tennis
  Players, 623
Improving Women's Running, 675
It's a Girl's Game Too, 668
Janet Guthrie: First Woman
  at Indy, 373
Janet Guthrie: Foot to
  the Floor, 342
Martina Navratilova, 364
Mary Lou Retton: A
  Biography, 379
Mary Lou Retton: Gold Medal
  Gymnast, 365
100 Greatest Women in Sports, 358
Perfect Balance, 355
Picture Story of Nancy Lopez, 375
Raising a Racket: Rosie
  Casals, 381
Softball for Girls and Women, 650

239

Very Young Rider, A, 362
Very Young Skater, A, 363
Women in Sports: Horseback
    Riding, 345
Wonderwomen of Sports, 361
World of Sports for
    Girls, 653

WOMEN IN TELEVISION
Breakthrough: Women in
    Television, 672
New Women in Media, 608

WOMEN'S HISTORY
Chinese Women in History
    and Legend, 646
Demeter's Daughters, 682
History of Women for
    Children, 152
We, the American Women, 651

WORK AND WORKING PARENTS
Ask Me What My Mother
    Does, 161
Going to Daycare, 165
Helping Out, 149
I Want to Be A Fisherman, 386
Labor: Contributions of
    Women, 604